"Such a great read [illegible] at really stick with you. I love hc [illegible] moments. It made me think, sm [illegible] in the world! A wonderful read [illegible] interested in leadership, self-awareness, and the messy, beautiful process of becoming."
Amy Williams MBE

"The book's mix of research, personal experiences, and thoughtful conclusions made me reflect on the deep fundamentals of life, our interactions within it and what really matters. A fantastic balance of light heartedness and open insightfulness. It gave me space to reflect deeply on my qualities, areas for growth, and the choices I can make to enhance my inner self. In the busy world we live in, making time for this personal exploration is invaluable."
Dr Michelle Penn

"Imposter syndrome be gone! This book is pure honesty - it made me feel normal and seen. It made me laugh and cry, and it really made me pause and reflect. It's inspired me to make some positive changes."
Mikhaila Found

"Smart, easy to read, and totally absorbing. This book is packed with powerful, emotional stories that made me laugh, cry, and reflect. The balance of serious messages wrapped in humour and heart is truly impactful. Perfect for anyone navigating change or feeling unfulfilled. Honestly, everyone should read it."
Jay Trestain

"I can relate to this book so much. At 43, it's comforting to read. Sometimes you feel alone in your experiences, but reading about others' life experiences that really resonate was so reassuring. Sammy's openness about her childhood, relationships, jobs, family, and more was both comforting and funny. I really appreciated her honesty and vulnerability. Heartwarming, funny, and so relatable!"
Pippa Flack

"I wish I had this book in my life years ago! It is such a timely and necessary read for so many of us right now. Engaging, inviting, and relatable, it's a tremendous exploration of what it means to be a 'grown up' in today's world. Sammy Burt is the perfect guide for the long and winding journey that so many of us continue to travel. I would recommend this book to anyone from the early stages of adulthood onwards - truly helpful for everyone!"

Ben Veal

"Everyone will relate to these deeply personal and human stories. You can't help but giggle, cry, cringe and arrive out the other side with a deeper understanding of yourself and of the rest of us! Sammy's characteristic humour and insight shines through!"

Juliet Daye

"As someone who struggles to read, I found myself gripped enough to read 8–10 pages at a time, that's 7–9 more than usual! This book is for anyone who feels imposter syndrome and is always searching for 'the grown-up' in circumstances rather than backing themselves. It offers a healthy, light-hearted yet supported look at how we all differ, yet match on so many levels as we 'grow up.' Raw, relatable, and thought-provoking, the author's own experiences enhance the content and make it even more engaging."

Megan Nile-Wills

"I loved the journey this book took me on. It felt logical but kept me captivated throughout. The use of stories nicely enhanced the narrative and made it feel so personal. At times, it felt raw with vulnerability and self-reflection. Sammy takes you on a highly personal, vulnerable journey told from many perspectives, rounded off with a lesson we should all learn from."

Lucy Collins

WHAT'S A GROWN UP ANYWAY?

SAMMY BURT

Publisher – Your Backpack Limited
yourbackpack.co.uk

Edition – First Printing

Cover Design and typesetting – Rich Carter at Rich C Studio
richcstudio.co.uk

Editor – Alison Waller at The Writing Path
writingpath.co.uk

ISBN number 9781738428700

Dedications

For my boys.

For Woody, whose imagination and energy inspires me to play.

For James, whose curiosity and experimentation inspires me to wonder.

For Jim, whose challenge and belief in me inspires me to stretch, and whose constant dissatisfaction with the world inspires me to act.

For all three lads, your humour and your love keeps me safe and sane.

Thank yous

Firstly, thank you to all the amazing people who gave me their time and trusted me with their stories. I learned so much from each and every one of you: Rus, Hira, Jay, Wayne, Sara, Sarah, Sharon, Lee, Cherie-Anne, Kay, Sienna, Vicky, and finally my Aunty Ann, who sadly passed away before this book was finished.

Secondly, an enormous thank you to my coach, editor, and friend, Alison Waller. Alison, you helped me find my voice and gave me the confidence to share my stories, research, and opinions. This would be a very dull compendium without you.

Thirdly, thank you to my wonderful parents, family, friends, colleagues, and clients for your constant support. Your shared hope for an answer to this big question reminded me that I'm not alone - and that this book might be useful to many.

And finally, the biggest thank you to my incredible partner, Jim - for giving me the time and space to write, for your unwavering belief in me, and for everything you do for the boys and I, every single day. I love you, I chose you - and, *you've done very well for yourself.*

Contents

PREFACE

The grown up game

CHAPTER 1

Heels and halloween masks

I am a nice person. I am a playful person. I find fun in all that I do. Whatever the situation, I try to 'make a game of it'. To an onlooker I am confident, carefree, happy and 'living my best life'. Privately I know that I am playing a game. And the game I am playing is one in which I succeed at life.

Like that's even a thing!

And even if that were a thing, to succeed at anything you generally need a measure of that success. Without one, how do you know whether to pace yourself or sprint? How do you know if you are on the right track or if you have veered off entirely? How do you know where you are headed?

One way to determine how you're doing, of course, is to look to those around you and measure yourself against them - to keep up with the Joneses. Is my car as new as the neighbours, are my kids as shiny as their classmates, is my Instagram as wholesome as all the people I follow? But the big assumption there is that success for them matches success for you - that you want and value the same things.

For most of my life I have defined success as being a 'grown up'.

I have worn the heels I can't walk in, I have nodded along to things I don't understand, I have come to work sick, I have stayed late. I have forced myself to socialise when I want to curl up and rest. I have sent Christmas cards to people I don't care about. I have made dull but sensible decisions. I have cried in the toilets - hiding my emotions. I have tried to embody what I thought being a grown up was and present it back to the world as authentic.

And it was exhausting.

While typing this I'm reminded of Halloween and wearing fancy dress as a kid. I remember putting on horrible plastic masks and feeling the condensation of my own breath on the inside - clammy and gross. The eye holes were so small and the elastic tight. I remember feeling claustrophobic, my discomfort hidden behind a playful mask that matched the high-spirited crowd around me.

Pretending to be a grown up was just like that. No-one could see me, not really, and I was so distracted that someone would see through my fancy dress that I stopped thinking about who I really was, how I really felt, and what really mattered to me - I just tried to make my mask a bit more comfortable. I didn't even try to take it off, just fiddled with it, repositioned it occasionally and, when no one was looking, lifted it slightly from the bottom for a breath of fresh air.

On the journey toward being a grown up we pop on these masks and pretend to already be one. To make matters worse, we are convinced that everybody else, everyone around us, is not wearing a mask - they are grown ups for real!

We kid ourselves that they have woken up one day with clarity of thought, sensible decision-making capabilities and 'grown up' wants and desires. They don't press snooze four times and then rush around every - single - morning - trying to work out where they left their shoes, coat or bag. These people don't want to eat fast-food and they certainly don't visit a drive-thru on their own, put the bill on their personal card to avoid conversations over the 'joint account statement' and then sit in their car quietly enjoying a cheese burger, before they head home for a sensible dinner. These people never ever want to strangle their kids, smash a mug, or scream at the TV.

These people...

Those people...

All the other people do not do these things or feel these feels because... they *are* grown ups.

And while we all know logically that these perfect people do not exist, we torture ourselves by projecting a picture of this character onto them. And because they are squirming behind their own mask too, they project it back at us, and the cycle of friendly deception continues.

I wondered if I was alone in wearing my grown up mask, but as I spoke with friends, colleagues and family, I realised that through nervous smiles and gritted teeth, most people felt they should be a grown up by 'now' - whenever now is for them. One person said to me that at 42 they still look for the grown up in the room when things get serious. More and more as I instigated conversations about this apparent measure of success, I found that actually it was a measure of failure. It feeds inner critics. It galvanises imposter syndrome. It is evidence to support any and all of the negative things we believe about ourselves.

As I wondered how damaging this mythical creature might be, I came across something that landed heavily with me. Something that led me to believe that not only have I spent most of my adult life striving to be a grown up, but that I spent most of my childhood in pursuit of it too.

Last year I was helping my parents pack up as they readied to move. They had lived in their house for 25 years. My four siblings and I had spent the best parts of our childhoods there and then returned with various boyfriends and girlfriends, eventually dragging the next generation along with us too.

I was boxing up my dad's extensive vinyl collection, dusty with a lack of play but dogged with years of love. Then, from between Dire Straits 'Brothers in Arms' and Pink Floyd's 'The Final Cut' fell a ring-bound wad of coloured paper. On the cover it read 'Bubble of Life - an autobiography by Samantha Jo Burt. Age 11'. Smiling with nostalgia I flicked through all twelve pages of this 'book,' remembering its production.

In our last year of primary school we were encouraged to write our life stories to date. We worked on them for weeks, producing pages filled with experimental fonts and Microsoft WordArt from the class PC, as well as painstakingly handwritten chapters with carefully drawn pictures. I read through pages about friends and sports, sections detailing my siblings and their various interests. One page was dedicated solely to listing my classmates' names. Once all our pages were finished, we marched up the corridor to the school office to have our manuscripts bound, making a record for the ages. Thirty-five preteens then proudly presented them to the school and our parents during the end-of-year assembly.

The section that really struck me was 'Thoughts for the future' and the tone of my eleven-year-old self.

'Thoughts for the future

I have a very changeable mind so what I may say now I may change my views on in later years.

When I was about 5 I wanted to be in the army. I wanted to fight with guns. As you may know I was a tomboy at this time, but by the time I was seven the novelty wore off and I changed my mind. I love animals, and like all the other girls in my class at the time I wanted to be a vet.

Usually as we do different topics at school, I changed my job ideas. It went on like this until I was eleven when I chose my job. At the moment (11.7.98) *I would like to study law and hopefully go on to Manchester University where I hope to get a degree. I want to be a lawyer.*

I'm going to have a big car too.'

Initially I laughed at myself as I read it. I smiled, recognising my desire for planning. I could see the qualities of me that are still very much alive today. My need to be taken seriously, my need to give justification and rationale. My belief that people will mock me, therefore I need to mock myself first. This has always been a default shield for me: if I point out how absurd I am, they won't need to say it and we'll be in agreement. As time went on though and I reflected a little more, I started to feel very sad for this young girl.

Now, at the age of thirty-five, I understand myself better, I know why I do certain things and I can often catch myself first, ask myself questions about my impending action and then make more conscious decisions. But this little girl, on the precipice of secondary school and teen-hood, believes she is self-aware. She protects herself with humour to deflect others' attention from her quirks. She tells people she has lots of friends and therefore doesn't need a best friend, to avoid admitting that no one has ever asked her to be their's. She tells people she is a 'tomboy', to avoid admitting that she would like to be more girly, but doesn't know how. She speaks to the dinner ladies, teachers and the parents of friends as an adult, to avoid being rolled in with the 'children' she doesn't understand and is so desperate to escape.

I was taken back by how I had distanced myself from any childish desires for the future. I would love to have discovered that an eleven-year-old me was full of big audacious dreams; of being the first person on Mars, or captain of the England Netball Team - anything other than this weirdly 'grown up' analysis of myself, my journey to date and my very exact and serious plan for the future.

Throughout the weeks that followed my dusty discovery I was often distracted by this little window into my past psyche. Again and again I read it and wondered why this little girl was so grounded and practical in her assessment of herself, at just eleven years old.

But of course I knew, I knew instantly really. I knew what she was up to the moment I turned to the page, while sitting in my childhood home amongst vinyl and memories. She was playing the grown up game.

She was already aligning herself with, and pretending to be, a grown up. She was trying to get ahead of her peers, under the false impression that maturity is a cake to be divided, so best get there early and grab the biggest slice. Believing the same to be true of respect and happiness.

Only over the last few years have I challenged those beliefs. I have entertained the idea that success, however we choose to define it, can be infinite. I have questioned what it means to be grown up. And so to the starting point for this book. I want to take off my mask, stop narrowing the world by playing the grown up game and instead broaden my world by playing in it.

I want to have an authentically fulfilling life, a life of joy. And trying to be a grown up all this time, without knowing what one was or how to do it, has been getting in my way.

* * * * *

In the 1837 tale, 'The Emperor's New Clothes' by Hans Christian Andersen, the Emperor is told by two very convincing tailors that they have the finest cloth known to man, a cloth so incredible and so beautiful that it can only be seen by the most intelligent and competent people - to all others the cloth is invisible. The Emperor, however, can't see it. Rather than risk revealing himself to be stupid or incompetent he agrees that the cloth is the finest he has ever seen, soft to the touch and with the most intricate of design and craftsmanship. But the Emperor goes one step further - he commissions the tailors to make him a suit from the beautiful cloth so that he may demonstrate his intelligence and his taste in one beautiful outfit.

After the tailors work for weeks on the invisible cloth the Emperor is presented with the finished suit. Of course he is incredibly complimentary of what he is presented with - as are all of his nervous courtiers. Everyone secretly assumes they are the only one who can't see the suit's beauty, they are the only stupid person in the room and so everyone plays along. Sometimes this is called GroupThink and in modern times it has led to some catastrophic accidents.

The Emperor proudly steps out in front of his people who have gathered to see the most beautiful suit ever made; but all they see are his tighty whities (I'm paraphrasing of course). In stunned silence the people watch him parade around the city. No one speaks.

Until a small child finally cracks and shouts 'He's got no clothes on!' The GroupThink is revealed. The child doesn't need to pretend that they are clever, they are just themselves and in doing so they expose all the adults, and the emperor, as frauds. The people laugh, the Emperor is mortified, and the tailors make off with stacks of money earned by taking advantage of fear and ego.

I think we can all succumb at times to the worried little emperor inside us and pretend to see or understand something we don't, for fear of appearing stupid or incompetent. In fact there are a number of unhelpful terms in the English language that, like the tailors' cloth, are spoken of with weight and authority but, like his suit, are just words with little or ill-defined meaning. Words that are often used without a great deal of thought, or with an assumption that they carry the same meaning for everyone. At best they are beige and empty, at worst they are a stick to beat people with - often they signify a thing to try to 'be' without any form or features to it. We all believe these words to have great significance and intricate designs but in truth, we can't see them - or at least, we don't all see them the same way.

The risk is we end up like the Emperor, nodding along wistfully with everyone else, agreeing enthusiastically and then prancing around in our pants. Well, maybe not in our pants, but we risk rushing around hoping that everyone sees in us something we don't quite see in ourselves.

'Grown up' is a wishy washy term thrown around as if there is a universal understanding of what it means - and I don't believe there is. The lack of a definition encourages us to feel like we will simply know when we have become a grown up, because we will be different somehow. We resort to 'faking it until we make it'. We pretend to be a grown up, hoping that tomorrow will be the day we finally feel like one. And, as is true in any situation where you aren't entirely yourself, pretending to be something you're not is exhausting.

The irony of the grown up game, and our belief that everyone around us has completed it and left us lagging behind, is that it isn't multiplayer. It can't be. There is no shared definition of the goal. And if there is no clear goal, no definition, then is there even such a thing as a grown up? This may all seem like theoretical rubbish, but our lack of a shared definition can be more harmful than we realise.

While I cannot, in one book, or in one lifetime, liberate us from all of the expectations we can be trapped and controlled by, nor can I fix a broken system alone, I do believe that to get anywhere we have to start somewhere. And if that starting place is to define what it is to be grown up, we can stop striving to be some cloudy, ungraspable thing and instead choose what and how we want to be. We can stop playing the game and start spending some of the energy we waste 'faking it' on the things we really give a shit about. We can stop competing with each other and instead create a more beautiful, more human and more realistic world - together!

In the following pages we will explore different contexts and different relationships in order to understand and define what it is to be a grown up. We will employ the robust research of academics and theorists, we will draw upon a survey of over one hundred wonderful people that I conducted myself, we will look at the opinions of children and dive deeply into the real-life experiences of some amazing individuals. And I'll share a story or two as they feel useful in answering our question - what's a grown up anyway?

INTERLUDE

Am I overthinking this?

Like many people, I can, at times, overthink things.

I remember being told often at school that I was 'overthinking' a problem or a task. Once, in a science lesson, I remember a jaded teacher lit up at a question I asked. It gave him the opportunity to explain to the class that what he loved about science was that it is the truest facts available to us right now, but that everything we believe to be true now could be disproven in the future - that science is a practise of investigation - not a wad of facts and figures to be adhered to. I will never forget the energy with which he told us how lightly we should all hold what we are learning and how we should never stop questioning what we are told to be true. I think of Mr Wilson often. But I can also still picture my classmates' stares of irritation burning into me like the tired Bunsen burners in front of us. I had taken him off topic, and he was a talker.

So sometimes this overthinking served me really well - I got somewhere more interesting or more challenging. Other times it got me into trouble. One such incident when I was about ten created a thorn in my side that still pricks me to this day - it was when I was shut down by a maths teacher. We sat in our rows in the cheerfully painted, yet well-worn Victorian classroom. Big windows to one side and the corridor to the other. White boards had just started to replace the dusty chalkboards and on our clean and crisp board in coloured ink were a number of questions. The question that tripped me up went something like this:

> *'A runner runs around a track three times. The first time she runs around it it takes her 10 seconds. How long does it take her to finish the race?'*

What the question wants you to do is to multiply the 10 seconds it took the runner to run around the track once by the three laps she needs to complete. 30 seconds would be the answer. Fairly easy really. My answer was 'around 30 seconds'. The teacher sort of grimaced at me and said 'Yes, 30 seconds.' I piped up again. 'No, it's probably around 30 seconds but we can't tell how long exactly.'

I got the distinct feeling I was irritating the teacher and all of my classmates. I could feel my body temperature rising at pace and my cheeks beginning to glow, as I had approached this differently to everyone else. I can feel my cheeks again now as I recall the incident. I often felt like the people around me wanted things to be simple - and to me, often, they just weren't.

Perhaps out of exhaustion, or maybe because I piqued her curiosity, the teacher asked me to explain. I told her that in the first lap the runner may have run fast, but in the second lap they might have been slower because they would have been tired. In the third lap they may have been even more tired and run even slower - although when they saw the finish line they might have got a burst of energy and run really fast, sort of evening out the times. This all made perfect sense to me. I wasn't trying to show off or be a smart arse - in moments like this as a child I was as confused that not everyone thought the way I did, as they were at the way my brain had whirred away.

The teacher exhaled with an exasperated sigh and said 'You're overthinking again Sam. It's just 3 times 10.' And she moved on to the next question leaving me in a thick cloud of embarrassment.

I'm sure the teacher was well-meaning and trying to make my life easier, but when I am low, or feeling unsure and self-conscious if I get a look of confusion or scepticism from someone, then that teacher's 25-year-old comment is as loud as if they were standing next to me.

What this situation, and many others like it, has instilled in me is a sense of self-doubt that I am overthinking or overcomplicating a situation. Over the years I have realised that while that may be true at times, more often than not I am just thinking about something from a different angle than others, or through a different lens. Gratifyingly, I have had a few occasions where I have been accused of overthinking something only to have the accuser join me in my complexity days or weeks later - once they have caught up. I don't say this to sound arrogant or judgemental of them, but I use these examples as evidence against the inner critic that tries to convince me to shrink back and stay quiet. My inner critic is called 'Samantha' - she uses her full name at all times. Samantha has been loud and lively as I've researched and written this book. 'Are you overthinking it? Surely it's obvious?'

It felt important, therefore, that I didn't skirt past something apparent and fundamental, 'overthinking' this whole attempt to define a grown up. So I started my journey in the most obvious place.

I suspect somewhere in my house is a tattered printed dictionary from school; however, I had no idea where to even start looking for it, so instead I reverted to Google - because Google has all of the answers, or so we are led to believe. I opened my browser and typed in 'What is a grown up?' I was uncomfortable. What if it popped up with a really simple and obvious answer? My inner critic, Samantha, was wringing her hands in anticipation of my embarrassing downfall, the words 'you were overthinking it' pursed on her grim lips. She is extremely tidy in her appearance - hair up, make-up perfect and lipstick applied in a way that I have never been able to master. Samantha stores up all the unkind things I have ever had thrown at me, all the mistakes I have ever made and regrets I carry. When she shows up, she tosses them nonchalantly in my direction with a power and pace that my inner cheerleader simply can't keep up with. She has a Rolodex of all of the things I have ever said or done that I regret and am ashamed of - she knows that Rolodex like the back of her hand. Samantha is very good at her job. Samantha is a dick.

I held my breath as Google loaded my answers.

The search engine started by suggesting other questions that are commonly asked in a similar territory. The first being 'Is it grown up or grownup?' which is a very good question and something I have had to take a view on myself. I landed on 'grown up' for the simple reason that 'grownup' looks to me like I have forgotten to pop in a space - simple as that.

The second question was 'What does it mean being a grown up?' As far as I know, Google's algorithms churn out the most commonly asked questions around your searched term. So, I am not the only one struggling with this question - many other Google users are too. That was a relief.

I scrolled on to the dictionary definitions to see if they would cut my book project short. The Cambridge Dictionary states that 'If you say that someone is grown up, you mean that they are an adult or that they behave in a responsible way: He seems very grown up for a ten-year-old.' This seemed a bit of a non-answer. It feels like a politician's response when pushed for clarity. I pictured a stout old man in a suit rushing this comment at a press conference then scurrying away from the journalists to check with his team if he had 'got away with it?' It says very little and certainly doesn't answer the question. My inner critic Samantha was squirming as my confidence grew - this wasn't a cut and shut case after all.

I scrolled down past bucket loads of unremarkable definitions that added very little other than highlighting the interchangeable nature with which we use 'grown up' and 'adult'. Eventually I came across a result from The Urban Dictionary. If you haven't yet crossed paths with the Urban Dictionary I highly recommend it. It is a dictionary built by contributors, where members of the site can add their definitions to statements or words. It not only has some brilliantly thought-through definitions but it is really funny too!

Many of its definitions related to 'grown up' include hangovers, which are referred to as 'grown up headaches', and 'grown up juice,' which is beer or wine. One user mentioned 'the grown up voice,' which is when a kid speaks with 'faked politeness... several octaves higher than their normal voice.' In my family home this was called the 'telephone voice' and as kids we all did it - in fact so did Mum.

I think my favourite contribution to the dictionary was from user Billy Magruder, who in 2005 added that 'the grown up' is 'the act of having or engaging in sexual activity: 'Tonya and I did the grown up last night." - I may have to bring this into my personal vernacular. If you go in search of the Urban Dictionary, do so with caution, as you may be shocked at what you find there.

Despite some funny but mostly frustrating and uninspiring answers provided by Google and various dictionaries, this search did deliver one thing - reassurance. Firstly, it reassured me that although we often use 'grown up' as a noun in conversations - 'be a grown up' - almost all of the dictionary definitions tried to clarify it as an adjective, a describing word - 'grown up voice' etc. We are trying to be something that isn't well defined as a thing to be. It also reassured me that there isn't a simple and obvious answer to this question AND that others are looking for clarity too.

While there may not already be a dictionary definition, Samantha hadn't entirely slunk off into the background but instead convinced me to bring some order to my exploration and encouraged me to look to the law.

PART 1

Looking for an adult answer

CHAPTER 2

Does the law know all about this?

One sunny August day when I was in my late teens, I mooched around the town of Rye with my friend Zoe. We had a pint or two in a couple of pubs, bumped into other mates and were generally having an uneventful day. My parents were away on holiday and this was the first time I had been trusted to stay home, mind the house and live independently of them - for two weeks anyway. As we wandered down the High Street with no real destination we came upon a tattooist. You can legally get a tattoo in the UK at eighteen and we had just 'come of age'. We exchanged a few excited words and headed in, ringing the bell above the door on our way.

Rewind four years and I was sat with my friends at the back of the old science lab of my secondary school, attempting to look fascinated by GCSE Physics. The headmistress wasn't often seen in the classrooms - or out of her office for that matter - so as she whistled past the window toward the science lab door my heart began to thump. Someone was in trouble, big trouble. I fidgeted with my skirt under the table and didn't look up when she burst into the room - probably the most obvious give-away that you've been up to something when everyone else's heads were up like a clan of meerkats. 'Look down, keep looking down' I told myself 'be invisible'. 'You two!' she bellowed toward our table 'I need a word!'. My school friend and I glanced at each other, and I suspect the blood draining from her face mirrored mine. We'd been found out - and much quicker than either of us had imagined possible.

Two days prior we had sat on a rickety train with some other friends on our way to Brighton for a day trip. We were all excited by the day ahead. Perhaps a little overconfident and rowdy; our energy and boldness powered by our teenage freedom. We were a tight group of friends, three boys and three girls. We were all completely consumed by the phase of adolescence when you are utterly lost as to who you are, and at the same trying to be your most tribal. We were working hard to be 'individuals' while of course being clones of one another; with our wide leg jeans, our grunge t-shirts, the occasional studded bracelet, or for the really brave, a dog collar - the look not complete without a minidisc player packed with Muse, GreenDay, and such like. I didn't exactly fit the mould - this was all new to me - but I was leaning into it with some baggy cords and a ripped t-shirt. I had moved schools and in my previous group of friends I was more of a 'townie' than a 'grunger,' choosing joggers, trainers and denim jackets rather than the all-black look I was now sporting. As our excitement for a day in Brighton built, we began talking about where to start - we landed on tattoos.

I had wanted one for as long as I could remember (which wasn't that long as I was only fourteen) and for months I had drawn a geometric sun silhouette over and over on any scrap of paper I could find - determined I would mark myself with it eventually.

My friend and I agreed that when we reached Brighton we would head to The Lanes (then a fairly alternative area of the city) and would get our chosen tattoos. The caveat we gave our fourteen-year-old selves was that if a tattooist asked for ID then we wouldn't lie but instead accept the inevitable and the endeavour would be stopped. We came to this agreement because we 'didn't want to get a tattooist in trouble for tattooing two underaged girls,' but I think we both secretly hoped that no one in their right mind would look at our naive faces and believe us to be eighteen.

We stumbled upon the only tattooist in Brighton who couldn't care less. In a dingy shop, wallpapered with chinese symbols, variations of roses and skulls alongside cartoon characters and big-breasted women, I straddled a tired leatherette chair; my back to the tattooist and my face staring at my friends in the shop through a dirty fish tank. I held my arms tightly as I lent on the chair's back, the fabric broken and torn to reveal the orange foam beneath. I felt sick - the kind of sick that is a curdling of excitement and terror.

When it was finished, my friend and I swapped chairs so that she could have something scrawled across her lower back - a much more public spot than the bum cheek I had just permanently marked! I remember rejoining the group in the front of the shop and feeling exhilarated. I was bouncing with the decision I had made and glowing in their encouragement and adoration. At that moment I wholeheartedly believed that I would never regret tattooing a large black sunshine on my pale fourteen-year-old arse. I believed I knew myself and the person I would always be. I basked in my grown upness.

When the head teacher burst into the science lab two days later my school uniform felt heavier than normal. My white blouse tight around my neck, my skirt long and immature, and my shoes bulky as they swung beneath me on my stool. Was I a grown up in child's clothing or, uncomfortable as it may have been to consider, was I still very much a child?

Needless to say, word of our adventure had moved through the school at lightning speed and reached the teachers before lunch on the Monday. The head teacher was less than impressed and the reality of what I had done and how immature it was sunk in as I pulled down my waistband to reveal the fresh ink to her - I felt like such an idiot.

Despite knowing that I would not choose to get the same tattoo now, I can honestly say that I have never regretted it. I don't love it, but thankfully it's never caused me any harm - it's well hidden. It is a thing that happened, a thing that I did at a young age - but it's not that big a deal.

You would think however that it might have taught me to give a little more consideration to how I marked my body and the lifelong decisions I make. This lesson was clearly heavy enough that as I sauntered into a tattooist on the spur of the moment again four years later at the legal and rational age of eighteen, destined to mark myself again, I had second thoughts. Those second thoughts however lasted all of two seconds and I left the shop with a spotty gecko on my hip. Said gecko is stretched and deformed now thanks to two pregnancies and resembles more Barney the purple dinosaur than the svelte lizard it once did.

Over those four years I grew and changed a lot but despite being able to show my ID and prove that the government thought me adult enough to get a tattoo the second time round - I still scarred myself with something hideous and ill-considered, then headed off to the pub to proudly show my friends.

While the world is beginning to open up to our teenage selves at eighteen and ask grown upness from us, we are nowhere near ready. We may be adults in the eyes of the law - but are we also grown ups? Or is that still a little way off?

Of course the legal age to get a tattoo isn't the only mark of adulthood in the eyes of the law. In the UK you can legally ride a moped and have sex at 16 - although I don't think doing both at the same time is recommended. You can drive a car at seventeen, and at eighteen you can drink alcohol, buy a lottery ticket and vote. At just ten years old in England, Wales and Northern Ireland you can be criminally responsible and tried in a court of law. At thirteen you can get a part-time job. At sixteen you can get a full-time job and, with your parents consent, you can join the army or get married. At twelve you can be trained to take part in dangerous performances - I picture riding a horse through a flaming hoop in the circus? - and at fourteen it becomes your responsibility to wear a seatbelt in a car or bus.

What a minefield of responsibilities. At ten I am seen as responsible enough to know if I am doing something criminal while it will take another four years before I am responsible enough to know if I have a seatbelt on or not? I can have sex and procreate at sixteen, bringing a child that needs caring for into the world; yet I cannot vote on the future of the country I bring said child into for another two years. And while I can have a child biologically at sixteen and am trusted by the state to look after it, I cannot adopt one until I am twenty-one. And when I take my biological toddler to the dentist for a check up I am still eligible for free child dental care until I am eighteen - so we can both see the dentist for free, mother and child. How lovely!

I remember a friend getting so drunk at sixteen that she had to go to hospital and have her stomach pumped. The irony being that she was on the children's ward for her recovery, surrounded by cartoon wall vinyls and brightly coloured toys. Her parents thought this fair humiliation for having drunk so much - in retrospect, so do I.

Historically, at twenty-one you received the 'key to the door', marking it out as a big birthday - it signified the start of adulthood when you could marry without permission, own land and write a will. But thanks to the Family Law Reform Act in 1969, which revised the 'age of majority' down, we can pretty much do everything we want to by eighteen - in the UK at least. Rather than the key to the door at twenty-one I should be given the keys to the HGV I can now learn to drive, handed the forms to start adoption proceedings or toast my eligibility to finally receive the national minimum wage! Oh yes, despite all the freedoms given to me, and all of the responsibilities expected of me by eighteen, I am not paid an 'adult' minimum wage in the UK for a further three years.

Looking around the world doesn't bring consistency and logic either. In the Philippines I am criminally responsible at fifteen but can't drive a car until I'm sixteen. In Japan I could get married at eighteen but I would not be allowed to toast my nuptials for a further two years. I can vote at sixteen in Brazil and Austria but not until I'm 25 in the UAE. In Canada and South Korea I can purchase alcohol at nineteen, while in the UK I can enjoy a glass of chardonnay or a cold beer with my parents from sixteen provided we are having a meal.

I am not taking a view on the ages at which we should or shouldn't be allowed to do things. I am not advocating for global consistency either, and while I think that perhaps some of these laws might benefit from being considered in relation to each other, I appreciate that it's complicated.

But what has become apparent to me is that the age at which we are deemed responsible enough to do certain things or old enough to have certain opinions available to us, differs a lot according to history and geography. The markers of my adulthood bounce up and down as I metaphorically travel the globe and shift contexts.

We may look to a legal age as a marker of a particular country's view of our capability or validity to be responsible for a specific thing, like driving, procreating or voting, but the law doesn't give us an answer as to what a grown up is.

So, the search for a helpful definition continues...

CHAPTER 3

Perhaps it's a rite of passage?

Growing up in a village with a bus every other hour between 8am and 6pm had its pros and cons. A plus was that all the kids in the village knew each other - you were stuck together and so friendships were born of necessity and grew into almost cousin-like relationships. A drawback, however, was a sense of remoteness from 'the real world' that took place in the surrounding towns.

This meant that we were all desperate to be seventeen, because at seventeen you could drive, and driving meant freedom!

I had been so desperate to get on the road that I booked my theory test for the day after my seventeenth birthday and studied hard leading up to it. I had already bought a small car, personalised it with cow print seat covers and sat in it longingly on my parents' driveway. I started my driving lessons immediately and like many other seventeen-year-olds at my college arranged for the instructor to pick me up and use the long journey home as a lesson. It was a picture of adolescence, the vast number of small one-litre cars lined up outside our college at 3.30pm, adorned with L-plates and leaned against by an array of instructors waiting for their students.

One day, when out with my dad practising, we had an almighty row about the 'throttle' and had to swap seats on the side of the road before he drove me home in silence. I had never heard the accelerator referred to as a throttle before and had no idea what he was shouting about as I stalled the car on a main road.

Another time, my mum let me drive to my grandma's house, which involved a series of large roundabouts near Eastbourne on our route along the coast. My confidence was more inflated than my competence was honed, and as I drew to a stop at the entrance to the huge multi-lane roundabout during rush hour, cars all around me, I casually said to my mum 'so what do I do here then?' Her voice squeaked and her eyes widened as she asked me in a panic 'haven't you learnt about roundabouts in your lessons yet!?!' To which I shook my head with a nervous laugh and proceeded to watch the traffic as if I knew what I was doing. We lived to tell the tale.

After passing their test, the instructor often takes the wheel from the newly minted driver to take them home: I assume this is because they may be excited and not concentrating, which seems very sensible. It doesn't, however, stop them from hopping straight out of the dual controlled safety of the instructor's car and into another one alone - ready for adventure! After running into my house to tell my parents I had a driving licence and receiving lots of hugs and 'well dones' I realised I now had nowhere to go. It was a midweek afternoon; seizing any opportunity, I volunteered to pick my little brother up from school. Perhaps not the inaugural drive I had dreamed of, but who cared. We cruised home together, taking an unnecessarily long route, both soaking up this new normal with music blaring.

Other than that, I think my journey into adulthood went fairly unmarked. I don't practise any religions so there were no spiritual parties for me to enjoy. My first job, washing up in a pub at age thirteen, merged into my second job at fifteen and into my third and so on. My first flat could have been a big moment, I suppose, but

I was always in such a rush to do things that it was quickly eclipsed by my next *incredibly important* endeavour.

And while many of my friends threw an eighteenth birthday party, I opted for something more low key. So low key in fact that I can't actually remember what it was! I imagine I would have been drunk, there would have been singing and likely the chain smoking of Benson and Hedges on a sticky dance floor while 80s classics boomed! I would probably have been in the basement club of my hometown, The Crypt, a club I had been going to for at least three years before I should have been legally admitted. So, the lines of 'coming of age' were blurred, or blurry, to say the least.

Weirdly though, I am someone who likes to mark things - I will celebrate anything normally. Which makes me wonder why I hadn't latched on to some big moment and carved it out as the moment I became an adult. It certainly would have fit with my constant desire to be one.

But perhaps people don't tend to plan their own gateway into adulthood. Perhaps by the time you want to be perceived as a grown up it's too late to then admit you aren't one and that you might have needed a recognised moment in order to become one. Perhaps to have planned a big 'I'm an adult' moment would have felt immature?

Lacking my own moment, and in search of the experiences of others, my friend Rus told me about his Bar Mitzvah, the Jewish male coming-of-age ritual, that happened when he was thirteen. The Bar Mitzvah (or Bat Mitzvah for girls) is said to be the moment when the child becomes responsible for their own actions, and when traditionally the father thanks God that he is no longer punished for this child's actions. I think my parents were being punished for, or at least paying for, some of my actions well into my twenties - transferring me funds when I was short for bills, helping me furnish flats and letting me use their breakdown cover, again and again and again. That aside I really like this idea that the ceremony not only launches the child forward but encourages the parents to loosen their grip in order to let the child learn from their own mistakes.

The ceremony takes place when girls are twelve years old and boys are thirteen, loosely coinciding with puberty. And while some Orthodox communities regard the Bar Mitzvah'd thirteen-year-old boy as a man in synagogue - man enough to count toward a quorum and to lead prayer - most communities see this as the moment when the children start *preparing* for adulthood.

However, as with most communities, religious or otherwise, these times of ceremony and celebration have multiple purposes. They are a time to bring people together, to put families on a platform to be admired, to demonstrate wealth and taste, to showcase children to others and ensure they are known and received in the community on their own.

Rus is an old friend of my partner Jim; they met when both were living and working in Kent and are addicted to each other's dark and sarcastic humour. I had put a shout out on social media to interview people who had been through a rite of passage or a coming-of-age-style ceremony. I then received a picture through my messenger. A picture of a young teen in a smart suit staring down at a huge cake in the shape of a scroll with '*Mazel Tov*' iced on top. It was Rus' Bar Mitzvah.

I was aware of his Jewish heritage, but we had never really talked about it. I had probably assumed that he was of Jewish descent, but as he didn't practice I hadn't supposed he had had a Bar Mitzvah or even been part of a Jewish community. So, when his face popped up on my screen for our scheduled interview slot I didn't really know where to start, so I asked him to tell me about the picture. By way of an answer, he asked me if I had seen the Adam Sandler film *You are so not invited to my Bat Mitzvah*. I laughed assuming he was joking - he was not.

The film, which stars Sandler's two daughters Sadie and Sunny, follows two best friends preparing for their big days. They attend other Bat Mitzvahs, all held in the same venue but with differing colour schemes, cake choices and DJs - all slightly tweaked versions of the same party. The room is filled with the same guests from Temple and follows the same order - readings and rituals in the synagogue followed by a grand entrance at the after party, food and dancing. In the film the girls have to attend lessons in the lead up and carry out a *tzedakah*, an act of charity, but their focus, no their obsession, is very much on the party and how to make theirs the best yet! Not a surprising mentality for a young teen.

Rus told me that his experience wasn't quite like that, but there were similarities. His family weren't particularly traditional and didn't attend the synagogue often, but his father thought it important that Rus and his brothers be presented to the community and share in its rituals in order that they had choices when they were older.

A 13-year-old Rus, who didn't have a single Jewish friend and was 30 miles from the nearest synagogue, was now attempting to learn Hebrew and spent weeks studying the section of the Torah that he would need to sing from on the day. It was both familiar and alien at the same time. Unlike the film in which many of the girls' friends were attending Hebrew school together and readying for their Bat Mitzvahs, Rus knew no one else who was preparing. At an age when you desperately want to fit in and have nothing about you that feels drastically different to your peers, Rus was suddenly different. While the preparations were thorough, the reading nerve wracking and the cake enormous, Rus didn't reflect on it as a big moment in his life. He recognised that perhaps for others it meant more, perhaps for some it did feel like a moment when their maturity could be recognised; but to Rus it wasn't. He didn't feel different. He wasn't treated any differently by anyone. Nothing more was expected of him. Like the party often thrown for a 21st birthday, it is a time to come together and celebrate, but not a moment of metamorphosis.

Maybe that's why many established rites of passage happen earlier in our lives, around the beginning of puberty rather than the end. Maybe, instead of marking that we have *become* an adult, they are marking the moment when we *start to more consciously prepare for it.*

This led me to ask a different question about what the conditions in which we begin to prepare might be? If we are looking for our caterpillar-to-butterfly reinvention - what kicks off the process, what starts our chrysalis?

To help me answer this I looked to English artist, writer and broadcaster, Grayson Perry who set out to explore the meaning of 'coming of age' as part of a documentary series on Channel 4 (which I highly recommend!). Initially he visits the Tikuna people of the Amazon as two girls prepare for their coming-of-age ceremony – the Pelazón. The Pelazon takes place after the young girl's first menstrual cycle and it includes various teachings, practices and a period of isolation in the days leading to a public ceremony.

The village gathers, decorates and cooks together, while the girls are kept behind a screen of palm leaves. The party starts to ramp up and a handful of men dressed as demons dance and emulate the dangers and temptations of womanhood. Entertained by the demons jumping and stroking hilariously long wooden penises, the villagers are whipped into playful excitement. After a while the atmosphere shifts slightly, and one demon moves from 'playful pervert' to 'playful, yet more determined, pervert' and begins to pull at the screen separating him from the girls, breaking it down with his huge bamboo penis in an effort to get to them. The girls are brought out into the melee, supported by female family members, where they fight and scold the demon into retreat, thereby demonstrating they are strong enough to ward off the unwanted desires and demands of men. In truth, the girls look like they have had a few drinks, and the fleeing of the demon is more symbolic than it is in reaction to anything the girls are actually doing. The girls then crouch and are surrounded by women who have been through this ritual before and know what is coming next.

The hair pulling. No, I am not referring to some chick flick scene where the girls angrily tug on each other's ponytails - this is serious. Every last hair on the girls' heads is pulled out, ridding them of the hair of their childhood and inviting the growth of the new hair of womanhood. This is a ritual you cannot watch without wincing.

There are many such rituals around the world. There are the land divers of Vanuatu in the South Pacific who jump from one hundred foot towers attached to bungee style vines, barely stopping before hitting the ground, and the Mepandes ceremony of Indonesia where the canine and front six teeth are filed flat as a way of ridding the individual of lust, greed, anger and jealousy. The indigenous Sateré-Mawé tribe of the Brazilian Amazon mark their boys' entry to manhood at thirteen with the use of Bullet Ants. The ants are collected and sedated by village elders, then sewn into the inside of gloves, stingers pointing in! As the ants come round from their drug induced naps, hungover and angry, the test begins. Each thirteen-year-old boy wears the gloves for 10 minutes, ideally without wincing or tears, demonstrating he is ready to be a man.

What I have found interesting as I have investigated rites of passage across cultures is my desire to have had one. Perhaps these ordeals speak to my love of a challenge, and my eagerness to be in a constant state of development. Because these rituals may be a privilege, they may be celebratory - gifts and adoration may be given - but they are also an event in which the child is vulnerable in some way and must survive. In all of these examples the 'child' is not just celebrated, they are tested, proving themselves to their communities. I enjoy the discomfort of trying something new. I enjoy high risk situations. I enjoy being celebrated by others for something that was tough for me to succeed in. So, a rite of passage would be right up my alley.

I am also drawn to the immediacy of the shift in how some of the communities around these children see them. You survived the bullet ants - you are now a man. You have had your Bar Mitzvah - you can now lead prayer. Your childhood hair has been pulled out - welcome to womanhood. But it is almost as if it's the people around these children who are going on the journey - parents, for example, having to change from 'having a child' to 'being the parent to an adult'. Like legal ages, rites of passage may denote someone as an adult in their community, but it does not mean that they are actually changed in any meaningful way. It does not mean they now have a definition of what it is to be a grown up to live up to or deliver against: merely that they have been invited to explore this new status.

So while I may now argue for the reinstatement of a rite of passage of some sort in my own community (with less hair pulling and fewer ants) I still don't think this is a marker of grown upness.

In looking for an obvious, even measurable answer I had come up wanting in law and rites of passage. That inner voice of Samantha was shrinking further as I stood tall with my view that it wasn't a simple question to answer. I pressed on. If the law couldn't tell us and it wasn't up to communities or cultures then perhaps it was something about the person themselves. Perhaps biology would round out my exploration...

CHAPTER 4

Biology's going to tell us, right?

The mating ritual of humans is wonderful and weird. We start it all so young, practising I suppose for when we need to play our part in the future via the next generation. Playing mums and dads with dolls before we've even started school. Then there are our awkward flirtations as young teens, still a long way from procreation itself.

One of the elements that unites the animal world is the risk of procreating. Certain male spiders perform to win the affections of a mate while, at the same time, they are unconsciously angling to be chosen as the 'plat d'jour'. Some snails are shot between the eyes with a sort of 'prepare to be impregnated' dart while many dancing birds are attracting both mates and potential predators in their efforts to be selected - hoping one turns up before the other.

One of the very first tricky situations humans experience when we more actively begin this journey of procreation is a long way away from the act itself. In fact I wonder if we are even conscious of what it is we are practising for when it begins.

Recently, I stood in the clammy 'games room' of a small campsite in France witnessing two such teens - and I both couldn't watch and couldn't turn away from the uncomfortable memories it brought up in me. The building was a large summer house, equipped with a pool table, table tennis table and various other 'cool' paraphernalia. The children holidaying on the campsite gravitated there as a place to be together and, more importantly, to be without their parents - I was cramping the style of every last one by supervising my two youngsters who were desperate to be involved with the 'big kids'. Most of the children were probably between seven and eleven and happily showing off their abysmal skills with a cue or ping pong paddle. All were French so, although I picked up the odd word here and there, most of their chatter eluded me.

The kids - mostly boys - were gathered eagerly around the pool table while an older lad of around fifteen or sixteen showed them how it was really done. He was the skinny, mid-pubescent son of the campsite owners. Polite enough when serving in the cafe and kind enough to entertain the kids in his spare time. His mullet was blond and wispy (why did mullets come back into fashion?) and his clothes fashionably baggy. He was cool, calm and collected - not showy or holding court with the younger children, but a leader of them with quiet confidence.

I noticed that the loud playfulness of the younger boys had subsided into a brooding quiet as they all emulated his manner. Then it happened. If this were a romcom there would have been some easy music playing and a light mist around his face, when *she* walked in.

She was around fourteen, I'd say. Long blonde hair, a white vest top and a denim skirt. She had clearly just popped on a little make up in her tent and brought with her a cloud of whatever body spray is fashionable these days. In my day it was 'Impulse' or one of what seemed like an endless catalogue of 'Charlie' sprays - I suspect Superdrug and Boots have moved on.

I couldn't take my eyes off of her - she was so incredibly nervous. Desperate to get the boy's attention and trying equally hard to be swallowed up by the nearest wall. Laughing at what was said and then correcting her volume or intensity. Speaking loudly and trailing to a whisper. Trying not to speak directly to him but definitely be heard by him. Her eyes moved to him about every five or six seconds. He, on the other hand, barely looked up from the table.

I was transported back to the youth clubs and discos of my youth, where I would have been that same nervous wreck, desperate to be noticed by the boy who had never looked my way. What I didn't see then, however, which I witnessed in the French games room, was how much he wanted to look up. He so wanted to laugh with her, chat with her, share a glance and yet he was as nervous as she was. His eyes were uncomfortably fixed on the table, unnaturally so. He was trying his hardest not to show her the smallest inkling that he was interested - and you only do that, or are that conscious of doing that, when you *are* interested.

These two weren't sharing this moment with any thought of having children, I doubt they were even considering sex. A snog or a hand hold would have been mind blowing, and at that moment, I suspect a lingering look would have sufficed. But I wondered how I would feel if I were single now, trying to get the attention of an attractive or magnetic person? I have gone through their stage, the pre-thinking-about-sex stage. I have gone through the only-thinking-about-sex stage. I trudged through the could-we-have-children stage and definitely don't want any more of them... so what stage would I be at now? Would it be the can-I-have-fun-with-them stage?

Only one thing was certain for me, as it has been true my entire life - I am cool as a cucumber around handsome men and beautiful women, until I realise I like them - and then I am back to being exactly like that self conscious, nervous wreck that stood across the pool table from me, just with a little less eye shadow.

While the biology for procreation might be ready for 'grown upness' at the age of thirteen or fourteen - the rest of us certainly isn't, and may never be when it comes to flirting.

*****

The textbooks I remember from school stated that we would be an adult when we had gone through puberty. After all, this is the point at which our body tells us we are ready to reproduce and by its very nature is ready to be responsible for the life of a helpless child.

Well, generally girls hit puberty in the UK between the age of eight and thirteen, while boys hit puberty between nine and fourteen. And for both sexes puberty lasts between two and five years. If finishing puberty is the mark of grown upness, then are we grown up at different ages depending on the length of our puberty? And if, on average, girls hit puberty a year before boys, are girls and boys grown up at different times? Are girls grown up before boys?

It's a fairly well discussed idea that girls mature faster than boys and I had previously put this down to the impact of society. I assumed that one reason of many may be historic expectations in the home, which we know still often play a part in family life; girls may have a greater sense of responsibility before boys. Or even that the trend of girls giving up team sports at around eleven while boys are encouraged to play well into their late teens may be because girls are encouraged to 'play' less generally, and this could be one of many reasons for their seemingly advanced maturity. Where does play go?

I assumed many contextual and environmental reasons for the perception that girls mature faster than boys - I hadn't considered it to be biologically true. In fact, it's not just that girls often get boobs before boys start to sprout facial hair. Research from Newcastle University hints that girls' brains may develop up to ten years earlier than boys!

I decided to look into the brain a little more in order to understand the engine we are dealing with here and if it, rather than the body, holds the answer.

Did you know that the average adult brain weighs around 3lbs and is made up of around 60% fat with around 40% of water, proteins, carbohydrates and salts? If I diet well I can lose 3lbs in a couple of weeks - I hope it doesn't all come from my brain! And although the brain isn't actually a muscle, I think it's useful to picture it as one that needs regular exercise and recuperation. I imagine it to be a muscle made up of neural connections, or synapses, which are basically the connection or joining of one cell to another. The string between two cups.

The Centre for the Developing Child at Harvard University says that 'in the first few years of life, more than 1 million new neural connections form every second'. One million connections are being made every single second based on the child and the environment they are in. This fact blew my mind - ironically! I have two young boys and no wonder they are so exhausted all the time. It's easy to forget that not only are they running around all day and tiring themselves physically but they are literally creating millions and millions of new understandings about the world every minute.

Initially, their brain creates simple connections and skills start to form, building over time in their complexity. This compliments a theory of nurture over nature. Imagine the brain of a baby being a blank sheet of paper, a piece of paper on which small dots start to emerge. And everything you say or do around that child, everything it is presented with or experiences joins up a few of those dots, over time building an intricate 3D dot-to-dot representation of the way that child understands the world and how they want and need to be in it.

And the reasons that the child will create the connections are driven by two human needs, needs that we are driven by every single day: a need to be in community and connection with others, and a need to survive. Subconsciously asking, over and over again, what will bring me closer to you and what may risk my life. Let's come back to that later on. If we were completely aware and conscious of all of these connections and how they influence us, if we were aware of all the decisions we make in just a single day we wouldn't be able to move from exhaustion. But thankfully our brain saves us from all that thinking.

We are only actually aware of around 5% of the thoughts we think. It turns out that our generous and amazing brains keep around 95% of our thoughts and decisions in our subconscious. My brain stops me from having to think about how to walk - until of course someone is videoing me and says 'just walk normally', then I have no idea how to walk at all. Their direction to 'be normal' moves 'how to walk' from my subconscious brain into my consciousness and I'm flummoxed. I have no idea how I normally place one foot in front of the other, I haven't considered it since I was eighteen months old.

At a certain point in life our brain goes through a more intensive period of development. Like a computer optimising, it removes connections that are rarely used in order to reorganise so that it may run more efficiently. Think deleting some files, putting others in an archive folder, and the ones we use everyday on our desktop for easiest access. And when this is happening it is a chance to revisit some of our beliefs about the world, to remove some connections and form new ones - for better and for worse.

This optimisation occurs between ten and twelve years in girls but between fifteen and twenty in boys, which fits with the perception that girls mature faster, both cognitively and emotionally, than boys - they optimise earlier. So, although the brain has slowed in its growth physically by early teens, the adolescent years are incredibly important for fine-tuning how it works and the files (or beliefs) that it keeps. It isn't until the mid to late twenties that the brain is fully developed for both girls and boys. The last part to develop is the prefrontal cortex - the part responsible for planning, prioritising and good decision making. No wonder our twenties are so much fun and yet full of cringe moments - we have the freedom to do whatever the hell we want but our brain isn't yet sorted enough to decide if we should.

Let's play it safe and say that most people's brains are fully developed, optimised and exercised to some extent by the age of 30 - does that therefore mean a grown up is someone over the age of 30 with a fully developed brain? Well - possibly? This might be the case but is it in any way useful? Without heading off to our local private health clinic for a number of brain scans throughout our late twenties and early thirsties - how will we ever know? And of course a brain being fully developed doesn't allude to the content of an individual's mind at all.

What this also doesn't account for is the neurodivergent. For instance, people with high-functioning Autism Spectrum Disorder (ASD) are often described as maturing more slowly than neurotypical people, but is that true or helpful? Are they just prioritising different neuro connections? This alone could be a huge topic and one I am nervous to reach into when I already feel that our question of what it is to be a grown up doesn't have a clean and clear biological or neurological answer.

Let's instead return to our games room on the French campsite. We have a young woman who is probably biologically ready to carry a child, whose brain may be in the throes of optimising, shaping and reshaping how it works and what it believes about the world, the people around her and even herself. We have a young man who may well be physically able to impregnate her but may not have even started his brain-optimisation. Both are yet to fully develop their prefrontal cortex. You can also layer on to this that in evolutionary terms the humans we see around us now have existed for a fairly short amount of time. Our bodies haven't had a chance to evolve as fast as our societies. Put simply, the age at which we go through puberty and ready ourselves to have children is probably more fit for a time in history when we didn't live as long, when we were expected to physically play a role in our communities much earlier and, of course, when more children died in infancy - so you had to start early and have more babies. Our bodies don't know that the average age of a mother in the UK in 2024 was twenty-nine, seventeen years after many girls start their periods.

So while biology may have some interesting insights into why we are the way we are at certain points in our development, it doesn't seem to hold a clear and helpful answer as to what a grown up actually is. To tell the truth I was a little relieved to realise this. I was drawn back to a definition in the Collins Dictionary which suggests that 'grown up' means '1. having reached maturity; adult. 2. suitable for or characteristic of an adult.' Initially, I thought the second point was as bland in its contribution as the first but I wondered if there was more to read into 'the characteristics of an adult'. I reflected again on the Urban Dictionary user Chalko3 who added that 'This is about the mindset specifically NOT your biological age. Grown ups come in all shapes, sizes, and forms.' Our answer wasn't found in biology, or neurology. It didn't reveal itself completely in rites of passage or culture and it certainly wasn't showing up clearly in the law - so it must be a little more complex than all that.

CHAPTER 5

Adult Vs grown up - why the confusion?

You can dismantle a jumbo jet.

There are roughly six million components that make up the Boeing 747 and, should you want to, you could take it apart and carefully lay out all of those pieces along a runway. The line of parts would stretch for miles and would no doubt be impressive in its order. You could, should you choose to, then put those pieces back together in a specific order and fashion and that jumbo jet would fly. (Don't try this at home). The jumbo jet is incredibly complicated but it *is* the sum of its parts. This piece, plus 5,999,999 other pieces equals a jumbo jet.

Eggs whisked together while steadily pouring in oil will result in mayonnaise. Some people may add a little dijon mustard or white wine vinegar but at its most basic, just two ingredients, eggs and oil, brought together using one process, will result in mayonnaise. It is far less complicated than the jumbo jet. And yet... unlike the pieces that make up the 747, you cannot reach back into the mayonnaise and pull out the egg. You cannot take the mayonnaise apart, see it for its parts and put it back together again. The mayonnaise is complex. It is more than the sum of its parts; its parts, when put together, result in a new and irreversible thing. A thing that no longer resembles its parts, but is something new entirely. If you had never encountered mayonnaise before and were given it on the side of a bowl of chips or in a sandwich and someone said 'you see that thick white sauce, how do you think you make that?' I suspect most people wouldn't know where to start in terms of ingredients or process.

The brilliant jumbo jet and mayonnaise analogy was originally dreamed up by one of the world's foremost complexity thinkers, Paul Cilliers. In 2014, when honouring Paul's life and work, Oliver Human wrote that 'complicated systems can be given exact descriptions whereas the complexity of a complex system always eludes such precision.'

Being an adult may be complicated. You can be an adult when you have finished puberty, when you can drive, vote or get married. You are an adult after your Bar Mitzvah, your confirmation or on your 18th birthday. There are many 'exact descriptions' that make you an adult; and they differ given the company, the context or the need - but they are clear. You can point to them.

Being a grown up is complex. It is something that emerges from a mixture of ingredients that may not be obvious and creates something new. We may sense when we are in the presence of a grown up but would struggle to point to the exact reasons why.

Perhaps this is a good time then to add two definitions to the dictionary: -

Adult
Noun / Adjective
Someone who has indisputably reached an adult marker relevant to the context of the situation or environment.

'When buying booze Justine showed her driver's licence to prove she was an adult.'

'Diego is an adult in his village having completed the Bullet Ant rite of passage.'

'Chandni's brain has developed enough to make her capable of adult thought processes.'

Grown up
Noun
Someone who... (Let's come back to this submission to the dictionary when we have a little more to say).

So, what are the ingredients that go into a grown up and who can help us understand how they are combined and transformed? Our exploration so far suggests that being an adult is measurable or traceable, but being a grown up is a complex mix of known and unknown ingredients, so where do we even start looking?

How might I work out the ingredients to mayonnaise if I didn't know what they were? By experiencing it! Its flavour and its texture, how it interacts with other things. I needed to approach grown ups in the same way. I needed to understand the flavours and textures of being grown up and the different ways we all experience them - and I needed to stay in complexity and resist trying to oversimplify this.

So we dive into complexity! And as the personal encounters with the law, the communal nature of rites of passage, and the risks and games of biology showed us, human growth could not be more beautiful, more messy or more complex than in our relationships. Through the different lenses of our relationships and the stories we collect along the way I hope we can surface some grown up ingredients.

INTERLUDE

Ask an adult

Professionally, I often design programmes or projects to help people get into quality conversations with their colleagues and I am incredibly lucky to have colleagues who, like me, see the benefit in collaboration. We are constantly discussing our designs, our approaches, or thinking. I am often not entirely clear on my own approach until I have talked it through with others. This is not because I don't have confidence in my thinking or because I'm lacking in experience or expertise, but because I find being in conversation with others the best way to articulate what is in my own head. That's not to say that I could be chatting to just anyone - in my working world I am surrounded by people who ask great questions, who challenge my thinking or want to understand my approach - these additional perspectives help me to delve deeper into my assumptions and my core beliefs, they help me to make my work more robust, and at the same time, remind me that there are multiple ways of approaching most things.

I know that working with others is incredibly important to me for my own personal enjoyment and in making my work as good as it can be, and yet...

When I began writing this book I completely forgot that key insight about myself. I went into my office, closed the door, put some music on and started hammering away at the keyboard, alone in my process and alone in my thoughts. I found it incredibly hard. No surprises there then.

It wasn't until I started speaking with others about their experiences, interviewing people, hearing their stories and discussing my thinking more freely and more widely that the book really started to come. I would never have bottomed out my theory, captured all this great stuff and presented it all here for you to read had I stayed alone in my dark room.

You'll spot quotes from the generous respondents of a survey that I ran and *we will meet some of the people who shared their thinking and their experiences with me in the following chapters; each and every one was insightful, valuable and beautiful - teaching me something that I continue to carry.*

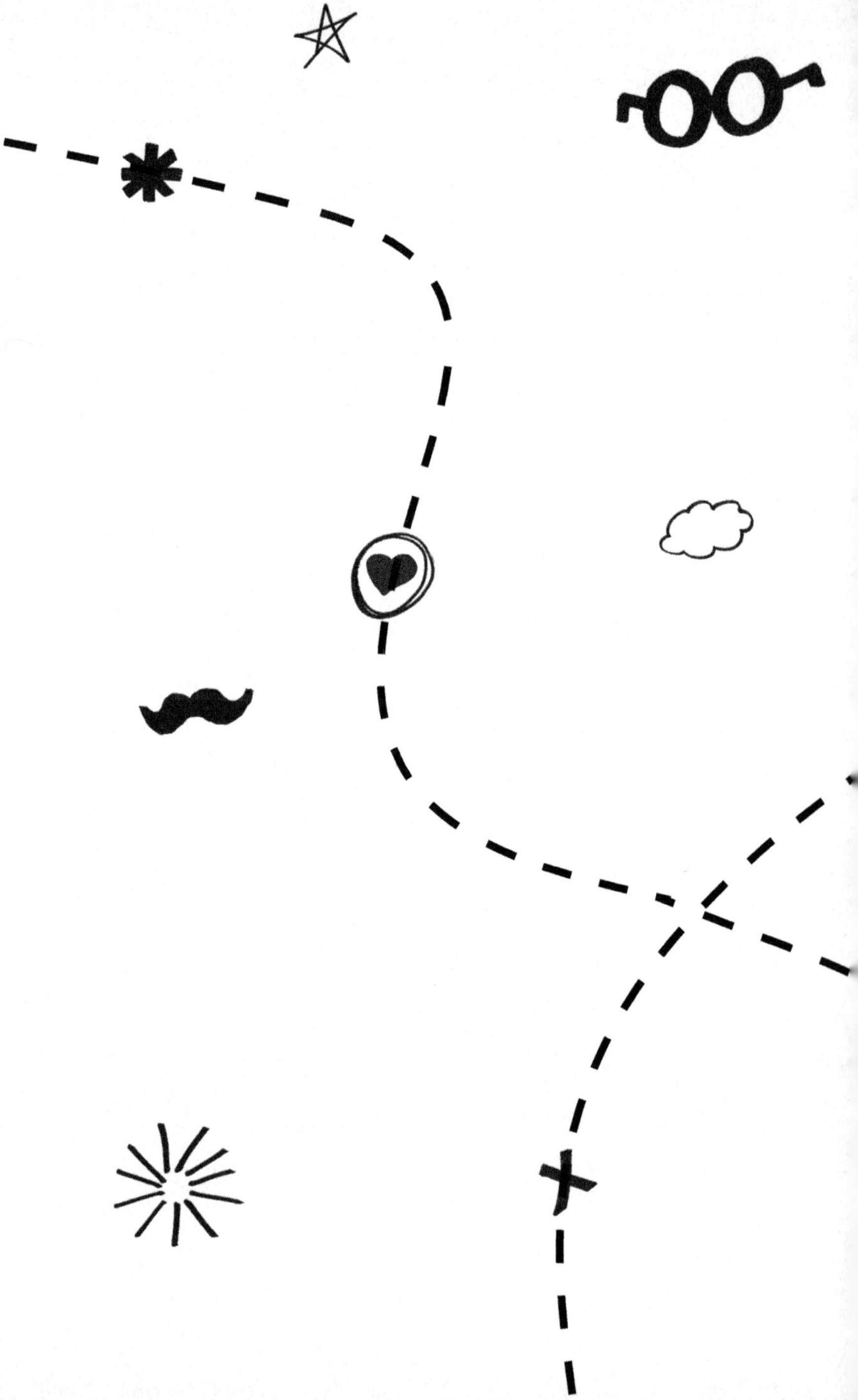

PART 2

The ingredients of a grown up

CHAPTER 6

What's love got to do with it?

**Picture yourself at around 10 years old.
What did you think being a 'grown up' was going to be like / meant?**

'I thought that grown ups were married people with kids. I just assumed that you got older, fell in love, had kids and that was it - not in a bad way but I didn't imagine it was much more complicated. How wrong I was!'
Survey respondent

In trying to understand grown up love I went searching first for poetic inspiration. I am a romantic at heart, and this subject drew me toward art before fact, initially at least. I landed on a web page titled '150 relationship quotes', and surprisingly it was a depressing read! Based on that article I have concluded that most relationship quotes have been coined by, or for, people who have had tough times in relationships and needed to know, in a poetic way, that it was normal. It was a bit like marriage counselling in bite size pieces.

> 'Assumptions are the termites of relationships'
> **Henry Winkler**
>
> 'Forgiveness is the oil of all relationships.'
> **Unknown**
>
> 'We are afraid to care too much, for fear that the other person does not care at all.'
> **Eleanor Rosevelt**
>
> 'Relationships are worth fighting for, but you can't be the only one fighting.'
> **Unknown**
>
> 'To love is easy, to be in a relationship is extremely difficult.'
> **Santosh Kalwar**
>
> 'Truth is everybody is going to hurt you: you just gotta find the ones worth suffering for.'
> **Bob Marley.**

While I don't disagree with any of these sentiments, I did feel that if I were an alien, just landed on Earth and my only experience with 'human relationships' was through these celebrated articulations,

I would happily commit to singledom forever. It sounds so painful, unrewarding, exhausting. So why bother?

Well for one, we are animals and therefore pre-programmed to look for community and connection in life, in order to procreate - and for greater safety and security. While these latter two reasons may be becoming less obviously important in our modern world, there is another reason that is as important now as ever before, maybe more... We need loving relationships in our lives for the good of our health.

In fact, there are mountains of research that show that quality relationships are so important to us that the lack of them in someone's life is actually a health risk. A risk comparable to smoking or alcohol consumption, and even greater than obesity and physical inactivity. Not having healthy relationships in our lives can make us sick and reduce our possible life expectancy.

This research doesn't just refer to romantic relationships or love, but to any healthy relationship in which we feel heard, believe our needs to be recognised, and feel supported and safe. Be that a sibling relationship, a parent, a friend, a neighbour, a colleague or a lover. 'When these [relational] needs are not met, we don't function as we were meant to,' Brené Brown, researcher, writer and theorist has said. 'We break. We fall apart. We grow numb. We ache. We hurt others. We get sick. There are certainly other causes of illness, numbness, and hurt, but the absence of love and belonging will always lead to suffering.'

I found this hard to read at first. It's weird to think that something that feels like a need of the soul or the metaphorical heart can have biological effects. And yet I've felt it. I've felt this when in unhealthy relationships. I remember feeling as though I would rather be alone with just the hope of love, than in a loveless relationship without any hope at all. It's made me sleep, and not sleep, eat and not eat, run and buzz and sit and wallow. Loneliness, or a feeling of being on your own, even when surrounded by others, hurts.

Most of the studies by academics that I came across in my search for existing research refer to a 'healthy relationship'. I toyed with this for a while - was this the same thing as a grown up relationship? I turned to the responses of my survey, which often referred to love and marriage - the qualities they described were uncannily similar to the elements of healthy relationships named by the researchers - so I've lent into this and paired 'healthy' with 'grown up'.

The adults who imagined themselves in their childhood shoes to answer my questions spoke often of marriage; of a wife or a husband, in terms of what they expected being a grown up would be. In some ways it formed part of the emerging list of 'things' grown ups have.

'I'd be married and have children of my own.'

'Being married and having children.'

'Being a grown up is probably being 'old' (over 25) and having a job, a house, being married and having kids.'

While some respondents wrote short stories of how they imagined it would be to be a grown up, for some it was their only answer, the only shape to what their futures might include - 'Married with kids.'

But before we consider this aspect of grown upness covered, I've been thinking about my own relationships - the good, the bad, and the ugly (and there's been some ugly!)

Though never married, I was engaged once, when I was nineteen. It was really an 'in the [drunk] moment' that got away from my then-boyfriend and I. We parted ways a couple of years later and I returned the ring. It was a lovely ring, but would not have been the marriage either of us wanted or deserved - our brains were still developing after all, and on reflection I barely knew myself back then, let alone him. I do, however, know people who met in their teens and are still very much together in their sixties and seventies, happy and content. So, I wonder if there is something beautiful and binding about finishing that prefrontal cortex development together, getting to know ourselves alongside someone doing the same.

My partner, Jim, and I are often asked if we will ever get married and I joke that 'it's a bit too much commitment given we only have a house, a business, a cat and two kids together'. I do this to match the lightness with which the question is often asked, and shift the conversation, quickly and without making the other party feel uncomfortable. The truth is; I think I would like to get married - but I am not sure if my reasons are good enough.

When I was young, I looked at adult relationships and saw them as unshakable, infallible, rock solid. This wasn't some idealistic hope but an honest belief. I always assumed that my parents were a team, that neither of them, nor any other married pair, ever felt anxiety over their relationship. I believed wholeheartedly that if you were married all the uncertainty over the other person's love and affection would have dissolved away with your singledom. I assumed that my parents had the same love for each other as we children had for them, and them us - utterly unconditional. I believed there to be a bond, some magical thread between them that could never be broken. It's weird because it's not like I grew up in the warm glow of some fairytale where Mum and Dad met at seventeen and never looked at another. My folks were both married before they met, as were many of my friend's parents - so I'm not sure why I felt this solidity so strongly. But I always felt like insecurities didn't exist for married people, and as I grew older and felt insecure in my own relationships I yearned for it.

I spent my youth watching Disney characters fall in love, dancing along with the men and women of old movies as they were consumed with a style of love that felt obsessive, addictive, and utterly consuming. I dreamt of the day 'my prince would come' and how my 'sassy attitude' and 'fierce independence' would captivate him - I was always more of an Elizabeth Bennett than a swooning Cinderella. He wouldn't be able to think of anyone but me, forsaking all others. I spent my teens, my twenties, and my thirties absorbed in romcoms and costume dramas where girls 'just like me' would secretly be beautiful, spotted by the handsome, aloof and powerful man, outed by him as the most wondrous creature on Earth and chosen, 'against his better judgement', to be his forever. Often I found myself drawn to the female characters in my daydreams - wishing that they too would see me as I saw them - something magnetic that I couldn't live without.

Even now I still want to feel that unshakable bond that I thought I witnessed when I was a child. I want to finally feel that I will be loved unconditionally, forever, by someone who, unlike parents, siblings or children, specifically chose me. Someone who cannot imagine their life without me in it. Someone who wants me to belong to them and to give themselves to me entirely. Not in a creepy way - but in an Elizabeth Bennet and Mr Darcy way - I wanted to feel completely safe - indispensable I suppose.

It's well documented how unhelpful this representation of love is, from Shakespeare to Austen to *Grease* and beyond. It has, for generations, sold girls and women a misguided idea of what a healthy relationship looks and feels like. I think in some ways this is why I have often had my head turned by someone arrogant, who appears to think themselves better than me – I want to prove them wrong! I want to be the Sandy to his Danny, and until scarily recently even the idea of entirely remaking myself for his acceptance seemed like a reasonable adjustment.

This fantasy hasn't done the lads any favours either, sending the message that men should be masculine, popular, secretly vulnerable and above all else – brooding or aloof. And don't get me started on its lack of representation of different types of couples and love! Even within hetronormative relationships you're unlikely to see a tall woman with a short man unless it's part of the storyline. Thankfully things are changing, albeit slowly, and the increase in healthy and happy same-sex and inter-racial relationships portrayed on TV and the big screen are increasing. A study in 2018 found that 'In the United States and beyond, few shifts in public opinion have been as rapid and widespread as attitudes about lesbian women and gay men.' The study reported that this positive shift was largely down to the 'imagined contact with characters in a TV show'. Essentially how we as viewers build trust and affinity with the characters, and how this can literally change the perceptions of an 'ingroup' about an 'outgroup' back in the real world. Unfortunately there are many people working hard to reverse this and create greater division and hate - but those people have no place in a chapter about love.

So, despite myself, the first reason I have always wanted to get married is to experience the love in which neither party ever questions their union again. In reality though I can't imagine there are many relationships in which one or other doesn't, at times, feel unsettled, unhappy or perhaps fragile – it's human nature - and a certificate won't help you avoid that.

The second reason for wanting to walk down the aisle, and perhaps a slightly more valid reason, is the party! I would love to have a huge party - to play the music we choose, to serve the food we love and to wear a real party dress! I want to bring the people I love together in one place and have fun together! I worry that if I don't get married then the only time this may happen is at my wake, and everyone will walk around saying things like 'oh, she would have loved this.'

Glib as this may sound, there genuinely aren't that many moments in life where we get to publicly celebrate ourselves. I didn't have a big eighteenth or twenty-first birthday party. I didn't graduate from university. I won't baptise my kids in any way. Maybe a wedding day is a safe place to celebrate our lives without judgement. Perhaps a wedding day is a day where we can invite love, support, and friendship, and indulge in it blissfully.

Jim told me if I want all that I should just have a massive book launch when this is finished - and maybe he's right. Or a huge 40th!

If I'm honest though, neither reason for getting married is a particularly good one. In fact, the first reason is actually a cop out for dealing with my insecurities, and probably means that I should avoid marriage until my therapist says I'm allowed! If I don't, then rather than be liberated of those insecurities I will likely spend the rest of my life wondering if we are still together because we wake up every morning and choose to be, or because we once stood up in front of everyone we know and said 'I do'.

It's Catch 22 - in order to feel unconditionally loved I want to get married, but if I get married and have a contract that says we have to stay together I'll have many moments of doubting the love.

I do of course recognise that a marriage certificate may give a different sense of togetherness than what I am imagining but I know it doesn't make us superhuman - we are still all capable of doubt, worry and betrayal. This is probably why most of the films I am absorbed by end on, or just before, the wedding - the reality that afterwards you are still the same two people, now without a party to look forward to and instead a mortgage and a 'bin night', may not garner the same viewership. Where is the tension? Where is the will they won't they? No, it is better all round if we imagine them riding off into the sunset for a future of bliss and obscurity.

I do have friends whose marriages are not all they were cracked up to be and rather than feel liberated of worry by their wedding rings, feel tethered by them. I also know people for whom getting married did bring a sense of stability. They felt it deepened their connections and their love. I know people who were so deeply in love that they physically ached to be connected to their partners by name, by law or by their Gods. And of course, there are millions somewhere in between, experiencing the mundanity of it all alongside deep and meaningful connection. Perhaps the two states can go hand in hand? Perhaps to stand the test of time, they have to? And maybe what marriage does also give people is a greater incentive to stick around and work at it when things get tough. They did promise to after all.

Hira's story

Having only experienced romantic love that was born of meeting someone somewhat randomly and initially, at least, experiencing attraction and lust, I wondered about love that starts in other ways and what we might learn from them.

There are relationships that start with shared intentions, or hopes, but no love or friendship to speak of. I thought of arranged marriages and wanted to understand them better. My naive assumption being that two people commit to marrying without having met much beforehand. That they and their families have agreed on their behalf that they will make a good match.

To be clear - what I am not talking about here is forced marriage, child marriages or similar. These are inhumane practices and have no place in our global society. No, I am talking about people who have willingly outsourced the task of finding a life partner.

I joined a Facebook group for people looking for arranged marriages, the perfect place to start. The group seemed to be mostly American, British and Middle Eastern people posting their pictures alongside fairly innocuous data - name, age, height, job. The majority seemed to be of South Asian origin, but not all. Their picture and headline data was then followed by a short list of what they were looking for. 'Intelligent woman, keen to have a family' or similar. The posts were mostly men and in truth the vast majority sounded like nice blokes. Many stated that they would like a woman with her own interests, hobbies and career - I wondered if this was being stipulated so often because they felt they needed to spell out that they weren't traditionalists hoping for the little woman at home but wanted to have interesting and equitable relationships.

I submitted a post to the group. *'Hi there, I am looking to understand more about arranged marriages and I wonder if anyone would care to speak to me about a loving arranged marriage.'* I started to get reactions to my post, but they weren't what I expected. Laughing faces appeared over and over until one woman commented that there was no such thing as *'loving arranged marriages - there were arranged marriages or love marriages. LOL'.*

I felt silly and misunderstood. What I had meant was that I wanted to speak to someone or a couple who were in a loving marriage that had begun as an arranged marriage. But others started to jump on her comment, mocking me and my ignorance. I tried to explain myself but it fell on deaf ears. I deleted my comment and left the group disheartened.

I was sure that there were many loving arranged marriages - otherwise why would so many people of my generation and the next, living in societies where it is not necessarily expected of them, be looking to their families to find husbands and wives. I remember a girl at my college talking about how she looked forward to her arranged marriage because her parents were so happy in theirs. As I searched I finally came across an article in the Independent called 'Why I had an arranged marriage – and it doesn't make me any less progressive' by Hira Ali. Grinning, I clicked through - here's my girl!

Hira wrote about the Westernised view of marriage and the hypocrisy often afforded to women about it. She described how Nobel Peace Prize Winner Malala Yousafzai was celebrated when she questioned the concept of marriage but dismissed and judged when she became engaged herself. We in the West want our female role models to be progressive but that often means only breaking with tradition - not deciding confidently and consciously to partake in it. Hira was a modern, successful and progressive woman who had decided to ask her family to help find her a husband. I had to talk to her. I tracked Hira down and messaged her - thankfully she was up for a chat!

A few weeks later, as I prepared for our call, I noticed myself feeling more serious than usual, my assumption being that I would soon be presented with a culture I knew little to nothing about, with ideas and ideals that I may disagree with, and that I would need to stay open and curious to them - giving her and her way of life due respect. I kept telling myself that she had a right to make her own decisions, like Malala does, and that I shouldn't judge. This need to coach myself was a response to the pre-judgement I felt brewing in me, and I hated it. My inner critic, Samantha, was running rings around me and tying me up in anxious knots.

Then Hira arrived.

She was a ball of energy and excitement. And, like others that I have interviewed, she just began talking. Her beautiful Pakistani accent paired with her energy and pace made it tricky to keep up initially, but it was clear to me that however her marriage had started, right now, seventeen years on, it was one full of love and admiration. I had absolutely found the right person to speak to and Samantha was silenced. 'Could we rewind a little?' I asked her, laughing. Hira spoke to me from the office in her London home, the background covered with books and I easily spotted a couple with her name as the author.

Hira told me about growing up in Karachi, Pakistan in a practising Muslim family, attending a Catholic school complete with Irish nuns, and socialising with people of all faiths and backgrounds. 'Because of my father's job we were lucky to travel a lot, at one point we nearly relocated to New York.' I felt a pang of friendly jealousy. My upbringing was fairly narrow in terms of exposure to other cultures, faiths and ways of life. Hers sounded so broad and colourful.

Hira had gone to college, then university for a degree, followed by a masters and was working in an HR role at a pharmaceutical firm in Karachi when she decided it might be time to marry. Unlike some of her university friends Hira hadn't dated at all growing up, she was laser focused on her professional future. So while she attended the weddings of friends in 'love matches' Hira seemed unfazed by relationships until her career was well underway. But at 25, a marriageable age, when her parents wanted to put the feelers out, Hira gave the nod.

I asked Hira if she gave them a list like the ones I had seen on the Facebook group and she laughed again. 'There were the usual things I guess. I wasn't too worried about looks but I wanted a kind husband. Oh!' she said giggling with a touch of embarrassment, 'and I wanted him to earn more than me. I earned quite well and it can be hard for a man whose wife earns more than him. I didn't want to be pressured to give up work or temper my ambitions.' I bristled a little, not that she wanted someone who earned well, but that she felt she may be asked to change if he didn't. 'I'd seen a few situations where the woman earning more became a source of tension, and I guess I was worried and trying to be cautious.' I noticed my irritation at a world in which we expect men to be uncomfortable with women's success. I don't think that it is as prevalent as it may have been for generations past but it is still there, and society and the media reinforce it regularly. She was right not to shy away from that - I loved her sense of reality. 'In hindsight, I realise that was a naïve ask. Income and earnings mean very little if there's no compatibility - and more importantly, if the person isn't kind and understanding.'

'It's a bit like modern day dating apps,' she said. 'Once the word is out that you may be looking for a husband or wife, you and your families might scope each other out at the events of mutual friends. My husband's family were introduced to mine through mutual friends who saw me at an event and thought I seemed like a nice girl. After that, casual gatherings were arranged.' This did sound like online dating - but better. It's 'datemymate.com' with way more context and research. 'So, Irfan and his family came to my house for tea.'

Hira had already met with other prospects and their families and had received quite a few proposals but she wasn't keen on any of them. 'They were a bit weird' she said, again laughing and enjoying the opportunity to reminisce. 'When he arrived though,' she continued, 'I was upstairs and looked down over the banister to get a peek.' She grinned at me and straightened herself slightly, seemingly preparing for something serious. 'My husband is very handsome,' she said, 'and so I saw him over the banister and liked the look of him straight away.'

'Sometimes these teas are quite formal,' she told me. The girls can be expected to serve the tea and stay quiet during conversations predominantly held by the parents. But Hira and her family weren't like that at all. 'I wanted him to see that I wasn't a quiet traditional girl.' But at the same time she was still a young woman meeting an attractive man for the first time with the prospect of getting together. So like any normal girl she got nervous and accidentally launched a samosa at him in an overly eager moment of attentiveness. I was enjoying the conversation as much as she was. It was just like having a coffee with a friend at the start of something special - she was sharing all the details with me, seventeen years on, as though it all happened yesterday.

Then the parents left them alone to chat and get to know each other a little. 'I don't wear a hijab to cover my hair,' she told me, 'but when there is the adhan, the call to prayer, I will lift up my scarf over my head as a sign of respect.'. As if divinely timed, the adhan began at the exact moment that Hira moved to pour Irfan some tea, the young host habitually covered her hair with the scarf draped around her shoulders. Worried this act may give him the wrong, submissive, idea she quickly clarified at a shy Irfan, 'I'm not putting this on for you!' Then, realising her sharp tone, followed with a smile and handed him his cup.

Despite having only known her for about twenty minutes I couldn't imagine anyone mistaking Hira for a submissive traditionalist. She was vivacious, ambitious, confident, funny and all the while respectful and gracious. Her energy was infectious and I nudged her to carry on.

After that meeting, Irfan told his parents that he didn't want to meet any other women. Although not conventional, Hira insisted on the two of them spending more time together alone. She had witnessed a bad 'arranged marriage' where the husband had cheated on his wife and treated her poorly so Hira wanted to test out Irfan and how he behaved with her in public. They had three dinners together 'and he was wonderful. Such a gentleman. We spoke a lot on the phone too and bought each other little trinkets, and I guess we were dating.'

'He bought me a red lip gloss on a trip to London which I have kept safe all of these years,' she said smiling, then laughed and added 'although I'm probably not supposed to use it now from a safety perspective!'

You'd be forgiven, as I was, for forgetting that this was a discussion about arranged marriage. This was just the story of two young people finding love in each other.

After they were married the two lived with Irfan's parents for a year until he was offered a job in Dubai and they had to start running their own lives. They had a son together and relocated again six and half years later to London. 'He promised my mum he'd never move us out of Pakistan,' Hira laughed, speaking to me from her London home.

Now with a fourteen-year-old son, about to celebrate her seventeenth wedding anniversary and her published books displayed on the shelf behind her, Hira seemed a truly happy and fulfilled woman. She told me of the differences between her and her husband. And how, it was in accepting those differences that they thrived. 'If someone invites us out or asks us to do anything I will say yes, he will say no and our son will say maybe,' she joked. 'That's how we roll as a family.'

Hira told me that she and Irfan had a love marriage. 'We told each other that we loved each other before we were married, so although the introduction came via others - like a blind date I suppose - and we agreed quickly that we would get married, the beginning was no less full of love than anyone else's.'

I had assumed, coming into the conversation, that there would be things that were initially awkward or needed them to work on but she batted away my questions. 'Like any marriage, it's challenging at first, living with someone you haven't known all your life.' I recognised that. 'Irfan and I have very different temperaments, and perhaps even interests, though over the years, many of our interests have converged. We've had our moments, and we still do, but thankfully, none we haven't been able to work through.' Hira and I acknowledged that however the relationship starts there is always something to work on.

'In fact,' she persisted, 'when my father passed away, it was such a difficult time for me, he was the only person I could tolerate around me. I have come to realise that in my lowest moments, there's no one else I'd rather be with.' That resonated with me too. While there may be people I turn to for specific support, when the proverbial hits the fan, I want and need to be close to Jim.

As I reflected on how Hira and I had compared her arranged marriage to that of online dating there was a distinct difference. Online dating is often about meeting someone to date, and so the bios describe how you may spend your immediate time together - 'I like to ski, I like to walk my dog, I like to travel.' but in Hira's case the intention was to make a life together, so the bio or brief included the type of life she wanted: children, work, perspectives on the world. Something about that felt more helpful to those looking for real, honest and sustaining love.

As Hira and I discussed all this, I told her that Jim and I had met on Tinder (a dating app) but how on our first date we had somehow got into the conversation of kids and marriage (granted we'd had a few drinks by this point). I made some off the cuff comment about wanting to have a stay-at-home dad as a partner and he told me how he'd love to be one. While this was lightly discussed and was probably coming from a mix of attraction and red wine, we were laying out some sense of the future we were looking for. Over the years we have had to work on our communication as a couple, what we understand and accept about each other and what we don't. We weren't ready for kids at the same time, have both suffered from burnout and overwhelm and have fluctuated a lot in how we look physically but, we have stayed in conversation about all of these things.

My initial assumptions about an arranged marriage being like a standing start where you immediately have to decide what to work on, put the hours in and hope that something great comes out the other side of it were, in Hira's case at least, entirely wrong. She had to put in as much work as I did, she loved as strongly as I did, she irritated him, I suspect, as much as I do Jim and their future together is dependent on their independent *and* shared happiness - just like ours.

At the end of the call I thanked Hira for her time and for sharing her story with me, and she thanked me for the opportunity to relive the early moments of her marriage. 'I shall go downstairs now and give my husband a big hug,' she said - still grinning.

I was warmed by Hira's story, and I recognised that love isn't all about marriage, and relationships aren't all about love.

Love can come easily, feel effortless and uplifting. Love can feel like something that defies logic and reason, something that emanates from within, but relationships, well they can be a little different. They can take work.

Sometime in the 1990s divorce overtook death as the main reason for a marriage ending. A number of things may have led to this shift. For example, divorce is now more socially acceptable, making it a choice that many felt they didn't have previously. An increase in life expectancy has also played a part, bringing with it a longer period of active life. The reimagined role of women in society is also perceived to be a contributor - women are out there in the world, experiencing new things, forming their own opinions, meeting new people and bringing all of that home and sharing it with their husbands. It feels pretty obvious that if both people, rather than just one, are experiencing things that might change them or their views, there may be greater potential for them to grow apart. And of course, the likelihood that both parties are working potentially increases the choices available to them financially.

However, a 2019 study at the University of Lisbon concluded that the main reason for marital breakdown was a lack of satisfaction.

Not groundbreaking as a headline, but intriguing. What does that actually mean? Well, the researchers determined two main buckets of satisfaction that need to be tended to, and that are often lacking in marriages that end in divorce: love and conjugal functioning (the way that we actually function in this relationship.). The love bucket includes things like feelings, emotional expression, sexuality, emotional intimacy, a sense of continuity and an opinion on the other's physical and psychological characteristics. The conjugal functioning bucket perhaps needs more conscious attention and regular consideration, and includes things like the roles we play in the home, how we spend our free time, how we are together and apart, how we have autonomy and privacy, how we communicate, how we disagree and how we have relationships with others outside of ours.

At first glance this feels like a lot to be working on all the time. I know of a couple who have an annual 'board meeting' - a time set aside for them to talk about how it's going, what's working, what's not, and so on. While they playfully use the language of business, they do actually try and put some structure and discipline around the time and its content. But of course, that won't be for everyone. I suggested we have a relationship board meeting to Jim after I heard about them and his reaction was less than agreeable, let's say. He already thinks I sometimes try to coach him against his will, and use too much 'business speak' at home. A board meeting about our relationship could, ironically, be the end of it!

Other studies have found that the romantic relationships that last, deemed healthy and enjoyable, are the ones where both parties continue to notice and are grateful for the other's contributions - however 'everyday' they may become over time. We want and need to feel seen and appreciated for what we do. When writing this chapter initially I skirted over the point about recognising each other's contributions to the relationship, but actually this is a huge frustration and pain point in many of the relationships I see around me, particularly once there is a home and kids in the mix.

And it's not just expectations between partners that causes friction. It doesn't seem to matter how many times we tell our nursery that Jim is the point of contact, that Jim is the lead parent, that Jim is the one to call when they need to speak to us - they always ring me, the mum. This doesn't just layer on unexpected and unnecessary stress for me, but it's sexist towards him. Of course this assumption that I handle all the 'kid stuff' doesn't come from nowhere. Despite both parents working full time it is often, but not always, the mothers in the relationships of my friends who handle the communications with school, are in the WhatsApp groups, arrange the birthday parties and plan the playdates. It's often the mothers who know where the swimming stuff is, remember the medications that need to be taken and pack the sunscreen.

On an episode of Fern Cotton's Happy Place, Gabor Mate, renown physicist and expert on trauma, childhood development, and stress said that '[women have always been the] emotional shock absorbers of their families, including their spouses' and that as women have entered the workplace and some of the chores, in many households may have evened out, the emotional load hasn't. It 'isn't often split evenly between the two people and therefore the woman often has two stress loads while the man has one.' Mate, even noted the correlation between rising cases of some serious diseases in women and the increase of women in the workplace - although of course correlation is not necessarily causation. This imbalance in the home is a sweeping generalisation and speaks only to heronormative relationships. There are many more men at home now than ever before, and many men who do share the load at home but the research does suggest that women are still carrying the greatest emotional load. I wonder if everyone has the potential to suffer in this brave new world - while I don't for one minute advocate for the days gone by where women would run the home and men would venture out to work - I can see that it may have felt tidier and perhaps less stressful.

There was clarity of who was holding what and, I suppose, clarity of what to appreciate each other for.

So, it turns out it's pretty important that we don't skirt over the appreciation and recognition of what each person in the relationship does. But what else did the researchers find was necessary in a healthy relationship?

Well, they found that a physical and / or sexual relationship is hugely important too, and within that a desire and effort to ensure the other person is satisfied. I read somewhere once that women in long term relationships are more likely to experience orgasms when being intimate with their partner than women in short relationships or with one night stands because the partner has a greater investment in their pleasure. This challenges the 'lazy husband' stereotype often portrayed in sitcoms and makes me wonder where that character came from? Perhaps women haven't always been honest about their needs in the bedroom? Perhaps a responsibility to female pleasure has changed over time? Perhaps it wasn't ladylike to speak up? Or, perhaps the writers of sitcoms just thought it funny to portray men as 'self-serving' in that department.

Another attribute for healthy relationships is alignment around values, something I was warmed to read about. You don't need to agree on every topic, you don't even need to approach things in the same way, but if your points of view come from the same fundamental values and beliefs you are likely to experience a synergy that binds you. If you both have an overwhelming need for fairness in the world, for example, then, even when your definition of fairness in a situation may differ, your intentions will mirror each other's, and with practice you may be able to discuss what you agree on as much as you do where you differ.

By this point I was learning a huge amount about grown up relationships, about the need for communication. The need for parties to talk to each other about themselves, about each other and about the relationship. Jim and I do do this actually, while it's not an annual board meeting, we do talk about how it's going, what we're enjoying, what we need more of, what drives us mad etc. Unofficially running an MOT on the relationship. But this has taken time, and requires both of you to have your own opinions - or at least to feel you have a right to one. I didn't always feel I had that right.

The bulk of academic studies into relationships suggest that love, alignment and shared values are important. Others discuss more formulaic elements, like similar backgrounds, religious beliefs and hobbies or interests and consider these to be positive contributors to healthy relationships. However, nowhere have I read any indication that the two people should become one. Sorry Spice Girls, but it looks like you were a little off the mark.

In the 1999 romcom, *The Runaway Bride*, Richard Gere plays Ike Graham, a New York journalist, who travels to a small town in Maryland to investigate reports that Maggie Carpenter (Julia Roberts) has run from the altar at not one, but three weddings - and won herself the title of 'The Runaway Bride' as she prepares for wedding number four. Ike sets out to uncover the story beneath the story and, with comforting predictability, falls in love with Maggie in the process.

With the previous grooms consisting of a priest, a poet and a motorbike-loving mechanic, Ike starts wondering about Maggie's choice of men. At each wedding the decor, the food, even her dress all resemble the tastes of the groom, rather than anything particular to her. Maggie herself seems utterly different with each groom. But at no point in the film do you, as a viewer, feel at all that Maggie isn't truly in love with each man. It doesn't feel that she is consciously pretending to be something she isn't but more like her shifts in style and energy, sort of, happen to her.

One seemingly innocuous but ultimately revealing question Ike asks as he interviews each groom is how Maggie liked her eggs cooked. The men each reply with, 'Scrambled, just like me' or 'Poached, same as me'. And when Ike and Maggie order breakfast while arguing over her life choices she follows his order with 'Oh that sounds good, I'll have the same.' In a passion-filled row where Ike tries to convince the fourth time bride that she doesn't love her next groom he says to her... 'You are so lost you don't even know what kind of eggs you like!'

Now I hope that you will forgive me for drawing a life lesson and literal moment of personal clarity from a romantic comedy, but enlightenment can come from the most unpredictable places. As I watched Julia Roberts and Richard Gere tussle with forbidden love nearly ten years after they first fell for one another in *Pretty Woman* I realised that I was just like Maggie. Not a prostitute turned serial bride, but a girlfriend that says 'I'll have the same.'

In all of my relationships I have unknowingly tried to be the thing that I think the man I am with wants me to be. I went out with a stoner and I smoked dope. I went out with a serious person so I became serious. I went out with a rugby player and I became a fan. I dated a funny guy, I tried my hardest to be a good audience. As soon as I realised they liked me and I liked them I began to shape-shift into what I thought they wanted. I would do anything I could to make them happy. I would go to the places they wanted to go, hang out with their friends. Try hard not to 'inflict' my personality on them but instead to emulate theirs. This obviously wasn't conscious, but when I saw Maggie Carpenter trying twelve different types of eggs in order to understand which she actually liked, a flood of understanding washed over me. I had no idea how I liked my eggs either!

And this shape-shifting is all about wanting to make the other person happy. Wanting to be the woman of their dreams. Other people's happiness has always been higher on my priority list than my own

- and I don't say that as some sort of humble brag - I now realise that I was never really making anyone happy, them nor me. These 'people pleasing' behaviours are actually a survival response - similar to fight or flight or freeze, which are ways that we have evolved to keep ourselves alive when we sense danger. This version of survival is often referred to as 'fawn'. To fawn all over someone, to put your own needs entirely to one side in order to serve them and make yourself indispensable to them. To ingratiate yourself with them, and do all that you can to make them happy. It's driven by an unconscious belief that if you are the thing that makes them happy, they will never do away with you - like sidling up to the school bully in the hope they don't turn on you.

Obviously, this isn't a particularly healthy approach to life and love at the best of times, but when you are with someone who suffers from depression, someone who, at times, makes you feel dispensable, taking responsibility for their happiness can take quite a toll - on both of you.

During our ten years together, Jim has suffered from depression a couple of times. When these bouts occurred in the first few years I became utterly obsessed with my mission to 'make him happy'. I would tidy the lounge, try and make him laugh, suggest idea after idea of things we could go and do. I would swim around him like a pilot fish waiting to spot a need so that I could swoop in and sort it for him. I would forgive him for his shitty behaviour in an instant, not protecting myself or holding him accountable at all. I would nudge him to move forward onto the next 'stage' of the relationship, be that a house, kids or marriage, in the hope that progress would soothe him as it does me.

I was so focused on his happiness that at points I was both suffocating him and pushing him away. I was exhausted. I felt unloved and without value. I felt like I was failing both of us and our relationship. I questioned everything about myself. And he didn't ask for any of this. He never once asked me to make him happy, to change myself or work myself into the ground trying to 'fix' him. And he was in no position to notice it himself and stop me. So, we bumbled along.

Over time the pressure built and I began to feel bitter toward him for his lack of appreciation and progress. Resentment grew and a heavy lump sat in my throat, often silently suffocating me. Then one day, while doom-scrolling on one social media platform or other, Will Smith cropped up. Now, please believe me that not all of my personal epiphanies come from celebrities or Hollywood movies - you'll find Aristotle in another chapter - but this time it was Will Smith. The post was a short video in which he said something like 'I am not responsible for my wife's happiness. I want her to be happy and I will try to create environments in which she can be, but I am not responsible for her happiness.'

It was then that I finally realised that not only was it not my responsibility to make Jim happy, but that it was a ridiculous task to set myself. I felt myself begin to relax a little. Almost immediately I started to loosen my grip on his moods and how I may or may not have been impacting them. I released my need for him to be happy, grateful or positive, about our lives together. I found a new comfort in the thought that if he wasn't happy in our relationship, maybe we shouldn't be in one. Not because I wanted to split up but because I needed to realise it was an option and that I would survive it. I liberated myself from a role as his mother, his jester, his nursemaid and his keeper and instead tried hard to just be me. And hoped that he liked that person, loved that person. It was risky, but a risk worth taking.

I tried hard to be supportive of him, be around when he needed me and not when he didn't. But most of all I tried to do what I wanted and needed, inviting him into my life and meeting him in the middle instead of always going into his. Or better put, recognising that we had two lives running alongside one another, crossing over a lot, of course, but two nonetheless. His life didn't have to be our life.

The impact was amazing. We are happier and healthier in our relationship than we have ever been. No more egg shells, no more permission, no more internal turmoil wondering what he's thinking - now I ask. We are having the most fun we've had since we met, we take the piss, we laugh, we are honest and we talk.

This takes me back to the '150 romantic quotes' I started with and to one from Carl Jung. This one resonated with me deeply: 'The meeting of two personalities is like the contact of two chemical substances: if there is any reaction, both are transformed.' I have unknowingly changed myself *for* others before and that's not worked out well, but Jung's thought that 'both are transformed' feels exciting, uplifting, and beautifully shared, but not owned.

Building on our learnings of two way appreciation, open and honest communication and conscious, concerted efforts to make the relationship all that it can be, maybe this is another component to grown up love, to be able to be in a relationship, and *be* yourself. Loving yourself as much as, or even more than, you love the other person. Giving without smothering, being dependable without being dependant.

So, while we've established that grown ups are connected to others, they can't exist in isolation, that no human can - I wonder how grown ups are connected to themselves?

CHAPTER 7

It's all about you!!

Picture yourself at around 10 years old.
What did you think being a 'grown up' was going to be like/meant?

'I thought I'd have long black curly hair which I'd always wear a pink flower in, and Jason Donovan would be my husband. Gutted none of that panned out. I imagined having a camper van and travelling around a lot and definitely never thought I'd have to worry about money.

I don't think I knew what job I'd have although when I was quite young I pictured being an Ally McBeal type lawyer.'
Survey respondent

While I have found the research for this book fascinating, it has at times been a little hard for me. It has made me consider myself deeply and at times I have been incredibly judgemental of my younger self - and my present self actually. I have scolded the seventeen-year-old through a thirty-seven-year-old's lens, I have scoffed at the twenty-two-year-old as if I should have known better, I have laughed at the child and her ignorance. I have been pretty mean to myself. And in diving into love and noticing the lack of love I often afford myself another layer of thinking was sparked, a question about how I feel about and treat myself. What is my relationship like with myself? And is there anything in that relationship that we can learn from?

In my research I asked people 'what trips you up most often when you try to be a grown up?' This question was purposefully broad, I really wanted to see what it ignited in people. Many said things like 'I don't try to be a grown up' but most often the responses referred to their view of themselves. 'My insecurities. My imposter syndrome. My confidence. My belief in myself. Getting in my own head. My inner critic.' Samantha squirmed uncomfortably.

We spend the most amount of time with ourselves, more than with anyone else on the planet. We are constantly hanging out with ourselves and in conversation with ourselves, so why is it that so many of us don't have great relationships with ourselves? I work with groups of people who, when asked, struggle to tell me stories of them at their best, struggle to tell me what is awesome about them - instead they easily find fault. Everyone can tell me how they can be better, few can reel off their good qualities. In case this is just because they don't want to seem arrogant I sometimes ask people just to think about their awesomeness - don't say it out loud but just tell themselves, in their heads, why they are fantastic. There is often a struggle even doing this and the voice inside their heads still prods on the bruises of their insecurities.

Why are we so mean to ourselves?

I am incredibly hard on Me. My aunt has joked many times that I 'should have been born Catholic' for all the guilt I carry around. And she's right - sort of.

When I am low, tired or stressed I dial up things to feel guilty about in my recent history and will go delving into my past to find something to berate myself about. I have sent emails decades after a tiny interaction with someone to apologise; often the receiver does not even remember the moment and thinks I am crazy - which gives me something else to worry about. In truth I don't do this as much as I used to but the habit still creeps in. Now I am trying to build a more empathetic relationship with my past self in which I forgive the nineteen-year-old that showed off at a party, and the seventeen-year-old who didn't really know how to have a boyfriend. I feel sorry for the nine year-old who tried to make her Grandad laugh by mocking him, and the twenty-eight year-old who was so had by imposter syndrome that she trod on someone else in order to be respected. I am trying to smile with the 35, 36 and 37 year-old who told the world her book would be launching imminently despite not having finished it, because she wanted to spur herself on.

And yet, despite all this forgiveness that I am exercising, the guilt and shame still creep in. The over inflated sense of how I *should* be, a responsibility to be at my best all the time, still clouds my view of the world. I even worry at times that I am not an interesting enough client for my therapist and that she may not be fulfilled by our sessions!

At times I take far too much responsibility for my clients, for my friends, for my family, for my colleagues, for my neighbours, for the person in the supermarket queue ahead of me, for everyone around me. And I don't think this comes from a belief that I am better or more capable than them. It is more a preemptive strike against the guilt that will come at me should I see or notice 'something' and not act. For example, if I notice someone's shoelaces are untied and I don't say anything, then they trip on them, I would likely take their fall as my fault - after all I could have prevented it. And I will feel bad about that for far longer than is necessary or helpful. My secondary worry then is that I am only doing nice and helpful things for other people in order to protect my future self - so am I a nice person, or am I incredibly selfish? I'll take that one back to therapy I think.

Me, and my craziness aside, I wonder how our relationships with ourselves, or lack thereof, impact our grown upness.

Cherie-Anne's story

In the summer of 2023, I sat down in a cafe in Bath ahead of meeting with Cherie-Anne, someone I had only met once before but had warmed to immediately. I was speedily scoffing a plate of eggs benedict before she arrived. I decided to treat myself that morning to an incredibly unhealthy breakfast because the following day I was starting a diet - again!

Footnote: I did not start my diet the following day - again!

Cherie-Anne responded to a post I had put out on social media asking people for their stories of 'becoming a grown up'. She felt like the story she had to share was one of not just coming to terms with who she is, but appreciating it, loving it.

Cherie-Anne started by telling me about her childhood and the annual conversations with her dad from the age of ten where they discussed her development, what she was going to need to work on in the coming months and what might need to fall by the wayside. These were not conversations about how she was getting on in maths or spellings but strategic catch ups to determine how she was managing the well-laid-out journey from child to next CEO.

Cherie-Anne left the home of her mum and dad and went off to boarding school at about the same time as these conversations started. Boarding school was a huge advantage in many ways: her education was second to none, she learnt independence, and she was always surrounded by friends. She was quick to tell me that she wouldn't change a thing about her childhood - it made her who she is. But as the eldest of two siblings and the daughter of a third generation business owner, responsibility was something that was instilled in her fairly early in life.

As she entered secondary school she was already conscious of the A-levels she would need to achieve, to study the course she wanted at the university best suited to it. She was focused on choices she would have to make at 13 about the GCSE's she would need in order to access these A-level courses. There was little to no wiggle room. And while on reflection this may sound quite overwhelming, Cherie-Anne admits that this was all very exciting for her. 'I was obsessed with long-term planning and the CEO position everything was leading to.'

I was reminded of the 'thoughts for the future' page in my own eleven-year-old autobiography. I suspect Cherie-Anne and I both strived to be seen as grown up and capable at that time - but I think she may have been a little more informed than I about what her future may hold. The picture she painted to herself and her father at that young age, of the successful female CEO, smashing business, leading others and being admired by all around, didn't, however, include her being gay.

We drank our tea and Cherie-Anne elegantly ate a huge cinnamon swirl as we chatted. I thought back to our first meeting during which she had spoken of her 'partner' in a natural and conversational way then straightened, looked at me directly and said 'I'm in a same sex relationship by the way.' I remember feeling sad that she needed to effectively 'come out' to me - that she didn't feel that it could just emerge organically. I paused and asked her if she has had to 'come out' a lot to people like that and to my surprise she told me that she does it almost every day. 'If I don't just say it, I'm worried they are distracted by the word partner, that they are no longer listening to me but just trying to work out if I'm gay.' She went on to tell me of a time at a networking event when someone literally just walked away from her after she said 'girlfriend'. I was suddenly aware of a privilege I am walking around with. I don't ever have to spend an ounce of energy worrying if someone will judge me, dislike me, or hate me because of who I love.

Surrounded by strangers but safe in the anonymity of the busy cafe Cherie-Anne told me how she had hidden her sexuality all through university: 'it just didn't feel right, it didn't feel normal, it didn't fit the mould.' It wasn't that she was ashamed of being gay, but that it felt like a complication in the plan, it felt like something that would confuse people or make them uncomfortable and she simply didn't want to be the focus of people's attention for anything other than her business prowess. Wrapped up in that was also the fear of rejection. As an 80's baby she had thrown the same insults around at school as I'm sure many of us did without really knowing what we were saying - 'you're so gay' or 'you're such a girl.'

So it's no surprise then that girls like Cherie-Anne grew up to hide their sexuality, and girls like me grew up to distance ourselves from other women we saw as 'overly feminine'. We're back to survival.

By her early thirties she was the business leader she had been trained to be. As a Director in her family's financial firm she won awards, often spoke at events, lived in a nice house in a beautiful city and was generally known for her cool head and business acumen as she networked her way around the business community.

Behind the scenes however things were a little different. Having hidden her sexuality all throughout her early career Cherie-Anne finally stopped side-stepping questions of her home life and came out at work in her third job. However, despite now being older, senior and in a loving nineteen year relationship, she was still too uncomfortable to hold the hand of her love in the street. She didn't want people to look. She didn't want people to make judgements or assumptions about her. She didn't want to make people uncomfortable either. She didn't want the insults she had received before to be thrown at her again across a busy road. She didn't want to have to defend who she was. And with nearly twenty years of practice under their belts, she and her partner Laura carried on quietly and discreetly moving through the world.

While keeping a big part of herself slightly veiled, Cherie-Anne was working every hour of the day, eating poorly and had a company of dependents looking to her for constant guidance and support. She was sick, on the verge of burnout, and something had to change. This successful and polished business leader was feeling unwell in a host of different ways. Bad back, headaches, tiredness, picking up every little bug, the list goes on, but she wrote them off to her work-a-holic lifestyle. The predictable outcome of dedication and hard work. I saw myself in her then too. I had often worn exhaustion or illness as a badge of honour. 'Getting ill every Christmas' I told myself proudly 'is just my body relaxing after months of being on red alert.'

Cherie-Anne assumed that decades of pressure and stress had led to inevitable physical damage that could never be undone, but unlike my badge of honour she carried a huge amount of guilt for having made herself so sick. She felt awful for the impact it was having on her partner and her friends. The guilt itself at times was crippling.

She lost a lot of weight and developed problems with swallowing food. She sought help from therapists, nutritionists, and doctors and received misdiagnosis after misdiagnosis, all the time losing weight at an alarming rate.

After two years of tests, lethargy and general illness, a private doctor handed her a diagnosis. A diagnosis that explained all of the symptoms she was experiencing. Cherie-Anne was released from the heavy guilt of overwork she had been carrying around with her by an unavoidable and totally freak autoimmune disease which caused her oesophagus to stop working. This was not a disease brought on by her lifestyle but something that she just had! She was liberated from the feeling that everything she was suffering from was of her own doing. She was free to manage her symptoms and continue with her life however she wanted. 'It was a huge relief.'

Cherie-Anne could be forgiven for returning to her high-pressured and fast-paced life once the symptoms were managed. The disease after all had nothing to do with that - and she'd spent her whole life training for it. But something else had changed. She wanted to feel different in other ways too.

'I started being stricter with my working hours. It was really hard but it had to be done. I had always enjoyed walking so I started walking or swimming everyday - getting out into nature and tiring myself out physically so that I would sleep even if my brain was still buzzing. I started to journal, to attend yoga classes and generally gave myself more time and attention.' Cherie-Anne said that while the illness alone wasn't the catalyst for her changing her life, it was a huge wake up call.

As she began to feel more herself for the first time in years, Cherie-Anne started to wonder how else she wanted to spend her time besides working, how she could use all of her experience, expertise and network for something that she really cared about. She became involved in an LGBTQ+ community. She's not entirely sure how it happened but once it started she found herself thriving in the connections it started to create. Yes, connections with the wider gay community, but she soon started to realise that she was also becoming a magnet for the straight parents of LGBTQ+ children.

Sipping her tea, Cherie-Anne looked coy as she told me of the conversations she was being invited into. 'I remember a father getting in touch - someone I had never spoken to before. He asked me what he should say to his seven-year-old son who loved his pretty unicorn dress.' We shared a smile for him. 'I told him to do nothing - just to be happy that he was happy. It was such simple advice but the dad really needed to hear it. I think he felt pressure from others to 'do' something so I guess I gave him some sort of permission to let him be.' Cherie-Anne looked embarrassed, like she was celebrating herself and wanted to back away from the limelight she was in. She really struggled to tell me this wonderful thing about herself without a shadow of shame. I saw myself in her embarrassment, and many other women I knew too.

Finally becoming somewhat comfortable in her own skin, Cherie-Anne told me how she didn't need to defend who she was anymore, the world wasn't asking that of her. Instead she could be entirely herself, and the world was benefiting from it. No, not just benefitting from it - they were loving it!

Despite never having really felt that she wanted to be different or 'more out' she found herself updating her LinkedIn profile to include a rainbow. She held the hand of her girlfriend when walking down the street. Her new found comfort inspired her girlfriend to start an LGBTQ+ group at her work too. And after twenty years together, they decided to get married.

Cherie-Anne described to me how she had gone full circle on the idea of marriage. As a child she had wanted to marry at some point 'like most kids do' but 'when I came out... Well, firstly it wasn't legal. But more than that it felt that if we got married, as two women, we would be making a spectacle of ourselves, drawing uncomfortable attention - It just wasn't normal.' She went on to describe how becoming comfortable with who they were closed that circle and shifted the idea of marriage from something *other* people do, to the perfect celebration of their love. 'And weirdly it felt so normal!'

As I sat in the cafe, welling up with tears over their wedding photos, Cherie-Anne told me that she never thought that she could possibly love Laura any more than she had before. 'After all that time together and all the tough times we have got through I didn't think getting married could possibly change how I felt about her, and yet...' she continued looking a little off to the side 'It did.' Cherie-Anne described it as another level of love - an upgrade! An intensity paired with a security she never knew she was missing. They were bound together now. And they were not only wrapped up in their love for one another; the part that shocked them most was the outpouring of love from their friends and families. 'All these people were just so happy for us - it was a real surprise to us that it was so important to them.' This 'love upgrade' seemed to be possible by Cherie-Anne loving herself more. Her acceptance of herself, who she was and not who she thought she should be, allowed her to love more fully, more loudly, more openly.

Now, Cherie-Anne works hard, but not too hard. She supports people in the LGBTQ+ community and beyond. She is even using her university hockey skills to coach a young team in her town. She celebrates who she is. And she has compassion for herself. She feels for the little girl who was so focussed on the woman she would be that she forgot to be a kid. She gives herself a break if she needs it. She proactively takes care of herself, making time to exercise - time to do whatever the hell she wants to do.

Cherie-Anne had spent most of her life trying to be what her parents wanted her to be, trying to deliver for her teachers, previous bosses, and her younger self. Striving to meet the expectations of all of these people was exhausting and 'if I'm honest, I'm not sure who it served outside of the day to day. I wasn't happy, and they didn't seem to care anymore.

But what I found fascinating was that when Cherie-Anne pivoted her attention inward, when she started to put herself first, she then had a new found compassion and energy for others. She had so much more to give! She was no longer serving others in an effort to garner approval and acceptance, no now she was thriving as a result of being there for others as her whole self.

Cherie-Anne made some pretty big changes to the way that she saw herself and how she lived her life, but it's amazing how many people don't change very much as they go through life - or don't believe that they do. A man in his late seventies told me that he was the same person now as he was when he was seventeen. My dad often remarks that he is still eighteen in his mind. But I often feel that I am a totally different person to the one I was ten, fifteen, twenty years ago - sometimes I feel like I've had an emotional growth spurt (or regression) overnight.

In holding this question of how grown ups feel about ourselves I came across an article in Psychology Today. The writer deemed there to be five personality traits that don't change very much at all as we move through life - broadly speaking. They suggest that they are:

- Openness to experiences: this includes intellectual curiosity and creative imagination as well as exploration.

- Conscientiousness: how we organise, our productiveness, and our sense of responsibility.

- Extroversion / Introversion: our sociability and assertiveness as well as how the company of ourselves and others fuels us or depletes us.

- Agreeableness: this consists of compassion, respectfulness, and trust in others.

- Neuroticism: our tendencies toward anxiety and depression.

Many psychologists now argue that these aspects of our personalities *can* change, but that any change will take a long time and is likely to relate to only one of these traits at a time. We may notice, when we look back over our shoulders to an earlier version of ourselves, that we have shifted slightly. I know, having been incredibly extroverted most of my life and fuelled by the company of others, that I now need a much more even balance of time with others and time alone. Too much of either is exhausting.

And it is useful to look back at the shifts we have made in our lives as proof that change is possible, because most people, when interviewed, struggle to imagine themselves in the future. In fact, Hal Hershfield, a Professor at UCLA, and his colleagues found that the brain activity when someone talks about their future selves is similar to brain activity when that person talks about, or is shown pictures of a stranger. His book, *Your Future Self*, is well worth a read. Loosely speaking, we consider our future selves as much as we consider a stranger, or perhaps better put - we have the same amount of connection to them. We don't see them as particularly different or similar to us; we just don't consider them very much. This means that when we make decisions that will impact our future selves we may not have them in mind at all.

Another study asked thousands of middle-aged Americans in 1995, how similar they thought their future self would be to them 'now', and then asked how satisfied they are with their lives. The questions were then repeated to the same group ten years on. The findings showed that the people who felt their future self would be quite similar to them had higher levels of satisfaction. Hershfield speculated that those who felt they would be similar in the future perhaps felt they knew their future self better - 'she is like me' - and therefore have a greater connection to them. He speculated that having a greater connection to a future self enabled people to make decisions that better impacted that self - leading to a more satisfied person as we trundle through our lives.

A similar study that seemed to prove the point was repeated in rural Kenya and found that women made more proactive and positive decisions about health and finance when they had been shown an AI generated image of themselves later in life. Having seen themselves old, and therefore been prompted to consider their futures, they could connect and humanise that future self, and make choices that would benefit them.

By being curious about our future selves we also make unconscious assumptions about their feelings. A study in 1998 by Gilbert and colleagues surmised that we imagine our future and past selves only to have the most drastic of feelings; that is, either utterly dismal and depressed or euphorically elated. This means we can often make decisions now based on a skewed view of how happy or sad we will be in the future. For instance, buying an exercise bike will be the catalyst I need for a healthy change. It will be incredible. I will feel amazing. I will wake up every morning eager to get on it and sweat out some calories. I must buy an exercise bike. The reality - well let's say it has been very different, but we do now have a cool place to hang coats.

Had I been curious about my future self at all, as if they were a friend, I may have identified that it wouldn't be the exercise bike alone that would entirely shift my mindset around exercise and that perhaps there are other choices I need to make first, tougher ones. But I don't always allow my future self, or my past self, an opinion, or a voice.

* * * * *

'Why would anybody be interested in what I have to say?' I sat on a zoom call with Sara, an incredible woman leading a company in the Learning and Development space. 'In my work, I literally support people to find their own voices - and yet I struggle to find or hear my own' she told me.

Sara appears to be an incredibly confident and energised person, seeming to bounce with energy when she is supporting others, sharing her expertise, describing a model or a theory. When Sara is listening to the ideas or stories of others she is animated and curious. She will riff off of their thinking easily and submerge herself in the conversation. To meet her feels like encountering a beautifully confident and considerate person. When the spotlight is turned on her, however, when she is invited to share her own stories, her own thoughts, she shrinks.

Sara and I hadn't spoken in a couple of years and we started our conversation with a bit of a catch up. She asked how the last two years had been. She asked after my kids, and after me. She was interested and asked follow up questions - I felt incredibly heard by her and loved the opportunity to talk about the boys and life generally. But after a while I started to feel selfish - was I hogging the conversation?

When I asked how she had been since we last spoke she responded with further questions for me, twice she did this until my third time of asking 'How have you been?' There was a pause and a nervous smile appeared on her face. She didn't know where to start, she looked around the room, searching for something - inspiration or solace perhaps - I waited. There was a deep inhale and then she began.

Sara told me about her business, things that were going well, she was learning some amazing things about their work and clients. Then she told me about a huge change in her personal life as she and her husband were parting ways. She told me about the fears she held and the hopes she had. As she spoke of this huge change I assumed this was why she had contacted me. I thought it was this massive shake up of her life that had ignited some sense of grown upness in her.

'So, is this why you wanted to talk to me about being a grown up? Because of your divorce?'

'Not really' was her still thoughtful reply. 'I'm sure it's in the mix but actually I wanted to talk to you about my childhood and see where it led.'

Sara started by telling me that she had grown up in a variety of places, moving around with her family from the UK to Australia and back again. Starting new schools and creating new friendships over and over again. She told me about reinventing herself in every new location, and the skills she had to develop in order to assimilate quickly. 'I would find out what programmes my new school friends watched on television and that would help me get into their conversations quickly. I would notice how they wore their skirts, their socks, their backpacks and did the same - mimicking what was acceptable and 'cool' in each school so as never to stand out.'

I was impressed by the ability this practice must have developed in her to make friends easily and noticed how easy she is to meet and be with. Then I noticed a guilt in me and hoped I hadn't created an environment for her to assimilate into when we met - I hoped she could just be herself with me.

She told me of the benefits of moving around, the friends she gathered, the different cultures she had seen and experienced, and the closeness she has with her sister thanks to their need to be a travelling unit. She described parts of Australia, a place I have never visited, and I became envious of her varied childhood. 'But always trying to fit in has its drawbacks,' she said. 'I think where I am most uncomfortable generally is in sharing my own stories - I just didn't practise it as a kid. I placed the value on being the same as the other kids in order to fit in and I didn't have time for my own individuality, I think I was scared of it.'

She remembered times as a child when she was told, while crying, that she wasn't sad. She told me how this made her feel confused. 'I thought I was sad but now an adult has told me I'm not - and adults know best right!?!' I reflected on the times when my sons fall over and I say to them 'you're alright!' in a very matter of fact, mummy-knows-best way. I winced.

'I think there is something about finding and owning your own voice when you are a grown up' she said almost to herself as she looked off into the middle distance. 'I think the phrase 'grown up' is used against children and then later against us all as a way of diminishing your opinion, your contribution or your story.'

'It's a moving goal post,' she continued, getting into her stride. 'The idea of being a grown up is kept away from you when you are a child and when you get closer to it, it moves again. We are told to 'grow up' without any support or guidance on how.' Her saying all of this was both reassuring as it's the whole purpose for the book, and sad of course that another person feels the way I do in this 'grown up labyrinth'.

'I love leading conversations in my work but that's because the conversations are about the clients, I just hold the space. But what's sad is that I also hold a belief that my stories are just not very interesting - and therefore by extension - I am not very interesting. Which all makes me wonder - why would anyone be interested in anything I have to say? So I keep quiet.'

This resonated with me so much - despite being a very chatty and open person. Even when starting to write this book I spent two years thinking it would be a book documenting the research and opinions of others. I saw myself as a curator, not a thinker. It was only when someone else pointed out that I had some thoughts and theories of my own that I realised I could have a role in the book. I could be a character in the book too.

Sara continued 'We tell people to 'grow up' whatever their age, which of course then makes them feel small. It tells them that we think they are childish or child-like - and that that is a bad thing. It is used to diminish our voices, our opinions, our stories.'

I was hooked on this thought train - if we are being told to be a grown up - because that is good, then by definition, the opposite of it, to be a child, must be bad? This may be true in an adult world at times but I wonder then if we are also inadvertently teaching our children that what they are now, a child, isn't good enough? They are born with a voice but our societal system quickly asks them to quiet that voice. We request that they listen, because adults know best, and that their voice is only valid or valuable at specific times and only with permission. We ask our children to spend years of their lives absorbing the knowledge of others, managing their voice and questioning the validity of their contributions. And then one day they pop out, we look at their 'adult' faces and we ask them what they think. It's like a nasty trick.

How should they know what they think! We haven't taught them to think, we have taught them to absorb. And we certainly haven't taught them to feel, to know how they feel, or to make choices about their actions based on their feelings.

So when we ask these new 'adults' questions that they can't answer and their voice disappears we tell them again to 'grow up' - the goal posts have moved yet again. We demand that they take accountability for their actions, for their development, despite having taken their agency away from them for years - and when they don't, or can't, we tell them again to 'grow up'.

When I have spoken to others, a sense of voice has come up a few times. People will describe someone in a meeting as being grown up because 'they don't say very much but when they do it's very thoughtful and intelligent.'

It took me a long time to feel confident enough to stay quiet in meetings rather than speak in order to have been seen to contribute. I felt that if I wasn't speaking I would be seen as stupid, lazy, disengaged. I would fill silences and garble answers quickly rather than pause, contemplate or admit to not knowing. There was a self confidence lacking in me that always felt the need to prove something. At the same time I would have an unconditional confidence in others that stopped me from correcting or challenging them - even when I disagreed with them. The two sides of this coin - they are right and I am wrong - then compounds the issue: if you see yourself as low in the 'credibility' rankings and others as high then the gap between you is expansive and hard to bridge.

It took me a long time to realise that when others deliver opinions with confidence and conviction it doesn't automatically mean that they are right - and that my difference of opinion is not just valid but beneficial to a quality conversation. So perhaps there is a faith that grown ups have in themselves at times; not a confidence that they are always right but an assurance that whatever their opinion, or question, or story, it is valid, that we have a good intentions when we share, or don't share and that what we have to say just may be of benefit.

In what Sara described, I got the sense that the voice she struggled to access, the stories of herself she fears are of no value to anyone else, is a voice silenced as a child. And now, she sees accessing that voice, using it and believing in it as the mark of a grown up. I loved how she was accessing it with me, how it and her opinion of it, was rushing out of her.

'I think a grown up is someone who has confidence in their own voice, someone who knows when to speak up and when to leave space for others.' She paused and we both sat with a satisfied smile.

'My voice *is* valid.' She exclaimed in a burst like it was a revelation - or perhaps a commitment to herself to use it. Her enthusiasm built as she raced into this crescendo of self belief. 'My stories are interesting to some people. My opinions are valuable to some people - but it doesn't have to be to everyone and it doesn't have to be all the time. It's up to me to choose when *I* volunteer it!'

There was a moment of silence between us again as we let the words land and then we both broke into laughter. We laughed at the weight of feeling and how it is both a revelation and absurdly obvious at the same time. But don't we often find that? We can say something to others easily and fail to hear it for ourselves.

Since our conversation I have seen Sara's face popping up on my social media much more than before, talking to camera and sharing her experiences, and hers is a voice to listen to.

And she looks so happy in herself, so happy sitting *with* herself.

Perhaps, what we are learning is that grown ups have quality relationships with themselves, they care about themselves - past, present and future. And what's imperative for those relationships is a friend-like connection with ourselves, knowledge and understanding of ourselves, and a faith in our future selves - so that we make choices and take action for their benefit too.

And, as we would with a dear friend, it's important that we protect ourselves at times too. This reminded me of a pivotal moment in 2015 with my colleague Geoff.

On a hot August morning, I stood in a New York hotel lobby with two colleagues. The lobby was polished and shiny, with inoffensive music playing quietly, flowers poised on every surface and uniformed staff stationed all around. There was a weird synthetic-ness to it that contrasted massively with the heat of the city outside; the din of the cars, the grime of the streets and the busy-ness of the people. The whole trip moved me in and out of highly contrasting environments and it all felt like a bit of a dream.

Back then I was part of a brand and culture agency, and we were starting to turn our hands to purpose - using our research and communication skills to help businesses understand what really mattered to them, and create strategies to live by it. For the few months prior to this hot morning in New York I had been working on a purpose project with the biggest brand I had ever worked on, and in a way that was more meaningful and more deeply considered than I ever had before. It was a real period of development for me - and I was loving it.

I was the project manager, the person responsible for making sure that everyone was in the right place, at the right time, with all the things they needed to make the magic happen. We were working with a huge drinks brand who felt their role was in bringing people together to have fun - we were swimming around in conversations of inclusion and exclusion, particularly around race and LGBTQ+. Over those few days we welcomed speakers who had fled their countries for fear of losing their lives - just for being gay. We visited community centres in predominantly black neighbourhoods and heard stories of great beauty and disturbing reality. We shared personal stories and experiences, visited art galleries and essentially submerged ourselves, and the group, in stories of being 'in' and stories of being 'out'.

This was all new to me. The brand, the project, the purpose and the potential good we could do if we got it right. It felt like a massive responsibility. I was leaving nothing to chance, and like Santa on Christmas Eve, I was checking all the lists twice!

My colleagues and I had flown in from the UK and two others had travelled across America. Five of us were about to start our second working day of six, with twenty-four of the brands' most senior leaders. One of my colleagues, a guy called Geoff, I didn't know so well. He had previously been one of the most senior people in Unilever, the parent company that owns brands like Dove, Knorr, Ben & Jerry's, Persil, Marmite and so many more. Geoff was the Global Vice President for HR. Geoff was a big deal. I was a little blown away by his experience and the work on brand purpose he had done at Unilever. I not only felt like the most junior person in the team but a little like I didn't really deserve to be there, sitting with people so intelligent and experienced, having conversations of such enormity. In my eyes this team was the epitome of professionalism and expertise.

I noticed Geoff taking a few steps forward and back on the marble floor that morning. He didn't seem anxious or concerned, just moving around a little as people do when chatting and waiting for taxis. His face was serious but not stern and his manner confident but not oppressive. He turned to my colleague Steve and I, and without a wobble in his voice or an apology in sight he said 'I am struggling with my mental health today and I need to take care of myself. I won't be attending the sessions and may catch up with you at dinner depending on how I feel.' He smiled at us both, and smoothly walked toward the lift.

I looked at Steve in terror. I had never seen anyone do something like this before. This was a really important day and he had a big role to play in it. At this time I was still absolutely of the opinion that the client was king and that the work should take precedence over everything else. Back then I would have been in the office with the flu, emailing clients at midnight and responding to unreasonable requests without batting an eyelid. My own wellbeing wasn't even on the radar. And this mentality wasn't forced upon me against my will, I wasn't forced to behave like this by awful bosses - this was all me. If I was going to deliver for clients and show everyone how dedicated, capable and grown up I was then this was just how it's done.

When Geoff excused himself from the day, I wasn't angry or annoyed at him, I was just confused. It had never crossed my mind before that anyone could step out of a piece of work like this in order to look after their mental health for a day. I was both stunned and excited by the prospect. Imagine having the self-love to make a decision like that!

And of course, it was no big deal. As a team we looked at the plan for the day, shifted things around a little, shared out the sessions that he was going to hold and life went on. No one died, no one got mad. That was also a shock for me. I thought others in the team may have reacted with an eye roll at least, or a full on moan about him at worst. But nothing. There was nothing. No drama, no frustration, no irritation. No one reacted at all - other than with compassion and understanding. I remember not knowing how I should react and watching others for cues. At twenty-seven years old I still didn't always have the confidence, in an unfamiliar moment, to work out how I felt before looking to others for guidance. I was very much led by what appeared to be acceptable or the norm to those around me - thankfully I had good people to follow.

Six days in New York in the August of 2015, talking about inclusion, exclusion, love and hate taught me a huge amount about myself and the type of person I wanted to be. It shifted my view of the world and of my part in it, but Geoff's two sentences, simple as they may be, encapsulated an enormous, and at the same time tiny, choice I never knew I had. I realised that I could choose to put myself first sometimes.

I could have compassion for myself, I could treat myself in the way that I would treat a friend, a colleague or even a stranger. I could tell myself to do what is right for me, something I had said many times to friends but rarely to the mirror. Geoff's priority at that moment was his friend Geoff - just as it should have been.

Geoff was a grown up.

CHAPTER 8

You've got a friend in me

What does being a 'grown up' mean to you now?

'As I grow older I find that I prefer genuine connection with people, I have less time for small talk or fair weather friends. Friends and acquaintances disappear from your life, days pass more quickly and you learn to nurture the friendships and relationships that are most important to you.'

Survey respondent

My son seems to have a different best friend every day. In fact, he has multiple best friends. When he was three, he would often come back from playing with a new child at the park and tell me they were his best friend - although he often couldn't tell me their name. Young children are experts at making friends, falling out, making up, switching and switching back. Their emotions go from truly hurt by an action of a friend to utterly consumed by love for that same friend in a heartbeat. Before the embarrassment or social norms of touching kick in, they hold hands freely, hug regularly and invade each other's personal space without an ounce of doubt.

These young children can make and break friendships over and over and over in a single day and still come home to tell me about their best friends. I am in awe.

When I was a kid, I wasn't anybody's 'best friend'. I was always included in the games or the parties, but I was no one's favourite person. As I entered my teens this continued. I was always invited along to things, but I would never have been a first choice or the reason a date or location was chosen - or so I believed. I had a couple of people who I felt incredibly close to when we were alone, but if a group should form around us then I would automatically assume others would gazump my priority position.

You would be forgiven for assuming from all of this that I didn't think very highly of myself as a child, that I didn't like myself very much; but actually, the opposite was true. While I was resigned to often being second choice I couldn't really understand why. I thought I was nice, funny, helpful and supportive. Often, I felt I was friendlier than the first choice of friend, and yet they always seemed to have something over me.

Now I wonder if I was the author of my own situation. Was I so insecure at never being chosen first that I was aloof and unreliable?

Did I flit between friends in order to keep myself from getting too close and being let down by them? Was I a risky bet for anyone to put all their eggs in one basket with?

This assumption that my presence doesn't really matter has bitten me in the arse a few times. I have assumed friends won't care and therefore won't be hurt if I am late, why would they? I am dispensable. I only discovered later that they had made a real effort for me.

When a friend flew in from The Netherlands to visit me while I was pregnant, I genuinely couldn't understand it. I always thought my value to her was in the fun we would have going out, dancing and drinking - I was a big pregnant blob, why would she possibly want to be around me? I was so nervous about her visit that when she arrived I didn't know how to be in conversation with her. I found myself overthinking every little thing - I had no idea how to be myself. I worried about how much fun she was or wasn't having, whether she was regretting her journey, if we were feeding her enough, if I was suffocating her, if I was entertaining her, if I was talking too much about being pregnant, if I wasn't asking her enough questions about her and her life. I can now look back at that visit as though I were a different person and see that she just wanted to hang out with me - lil' ol' me.

At thirty-seven I sometimes find friendships quite hard. I don't always understand them. I don't know what the rules are, or the boundaries so I often flounder in them, misreading the other person or the situation and feeling either like I have let someone down or that I have been rejected by them. In fact, I would go so far as to say that throughout my life I have been more insecure in my friendships than in any other relationships. In truth, part of this is because I don't think I am, or have ever been 'cool' - I have never been particularly fashionable in my clothes, I rarely listen to the 'right' music, and I don't seem to be into things at the same time that other people are, getting to them well before or well after they do. Take my friend from the Netherlands - she's so cool. A DJ, a writer, a cooler than cool dresser with a take no shit attitude that I have always been jealous of. Why would she possibly want to hang out with me?

On the radio recently I heard a woman speaking about how she, her husband and baby had moved to the same city as her best friend when they returned from living abroad. Of all the places in the UK they could have chosen, and all the reasons to choose them - family, work, culture, and so on - they chose the city that her best friend lived in in order to be close to her.

I was intrigued by this. And the reason was that I cannot personally imagine being so comfortable in a friendship that I would make that decision. I would be terrified that I was misreading the level of our friendship, that I was 'following' someone who may not want to be followed. I would be terrified that should I move near them they would feel obliged to bring me into their social circles and their hobbies. I would be so worried that by moving near to them I would appear overly keen, without my own direction or interests, and become a burden to this friend. A hanger on.

I would love to feel so safe in a friendship that I could even invite myself to someone's party, let alone their hometown. As I write this I do find it sad, and I am challenging myself around its truth. Am I being overly dramatic here? I don't think so.

Now I do have friends who I could text and say 'hey shall we find a date for dinner' or similar, but I will always leave it open enough that should they want to back away they can do – without awkwardness on anyone's part. I always give them a way to get out of it, a way to say no. Aside from my low scores on the 'cool-o-meter' this also stems from a belief that unless I am of value to someone else in some way then others wouldn't choose to be around me. I guess I just don't really know how to hang out - and the suggestion of it can fill me with dread.

Give me a job however and I am away!

- Come over and help me with my website - I'm in!

- Pop round and let's talk about what's bothering me - no worries!

- Swing by and borrow an onion, an iron, a bottle of wine - sorted!

- Hang out - ummmm for what purpose?

I do have a group of friends who I met through antenatal classes before having our first children and with them I can hang out. I can meet up without an agenda, I can be myself, I can sit quietly, or I can be the life and soul. I don't need to put on a pretence. I can cry with them; I can confide in them. They have looked after my kids and I theirs. They have seen my house at its worst and know some of my most intimate and gross truths.

Is this because we went through something life changing within days of each other and therefore have built some unnameable bond; or was I lucky enough to accidentally procreate at the same time as a group of strangers I was destined to meet? Who knows!

Perhaps going through something at the same time did give us a reason to be friends. It gave me a boundary or some security for why they would want to be around me. And, over time, as the kids have grown and lives have got busier, our constant endeavours to meet up, even for half an hour here and there, have given me the confidence to trust them, and to believe that they love me, for who I am, not what I can bring to the relationship.

I recently messaged this group in a moment of utter vulnerability and, based on the intimacy we share, said 'Hey guys - I think I need to be near you all soon.' I could have used 'catch up' by way of more acceptable code but for whatever reason I actually didn't care if we exchanged our latest stories or compared our life notes - I just wanted to be close to them and feel safe in company. 'I need to be near you too!' came one person within seconds. Phew!

Sharon's story

Sharon was introduced to me through a mutual friend - and she was everything she was promised to be. A compliment giving, 'your shoelace is untied' telling, straight talking, contagiously laughing, friend making machine. Sharon reminded me of one of my oldest friends - someone who is utterly magnetic. It's impossible for her to leave the house without bumping into someone who wants to spend time with her, be near her. What I have noticed over the years however is that not all of these people are good for her. They don't want to be a friend to her, they don't want her when she's low or quiet. They want her when she is the gregarious, attention pulling catalyst of fun times - they want the character, not the person.

Often before an interview I have a call with the interviewee. A way of giving them shape and safety in what I am up to and what I may do with their story - I guess I don't assume they have the same instant trust in me as I do in them. With Sharon - no precall was needed. I rang her at our agreed time, and we were off, straight in there to the good stuff - she chose to trust me straight away too. No small talk, no chit chat. She just started telling me about her life - once again I felt so grateful for this book's excuse to speak with people! She was a high energy speed talker - I rushed to start my laptop recording so as not to miss a beat and then relaxed into what was a revitalising conversation. In 43 minutes there were laughs, tears and frustrations - it was beautiful.

Sharon is a 59 year-old woman living very close to my home town with her husband and dog. She's worked in the probation service for 25 years and has been a sportswoman for the majority of her life - which plays havoc with her knees these days, 'but that's to be expected' she said.

'I spent most of my time outside the classroom when I was at school,' she told me. 'Not because I was naughty as such but I was bored.' Sharon reflected on the way she was taught in the eighties. 'I was talked at for three hours at a time, not asked any questions, shown barely any demonstrations, nothing to get involved with - it was boring. And when the teacher asked why I wasn't paying attention I tended to tell them the truth. Hence sitting outside the classroom rather than in it.' I pictured a young punky Sharon on a wooden chair in a corridor swinging her legs and staring at the ceiling with utter disinterest - although actually I had no idea what Sharon looked like as we'd taken to having a voice call rather than video.

Sharon told me that her school report said she would never make anything of herself. She said that she mostly felt like a problem and an inconvenience. She couldn't do things the way others did, she didn't want to. Her way was always different but it made sense to her - so she stuck with it. Her brain was constantly multitasking and trying to focus on a single thing was both unrealistic and exhausting.

As Sharon grew and entered her teens, this confident sense of self gave way to the social pressure of life and she began playing a role - in her social world at least, school was still tricky. 'I am a brilliant masker,' she told me. 'I got through life by being a bit cheeky, quite good at sports, and building resilience in how I should navigate this quite challenging world.'

This sense of difference and quick thinking, alongside a desire to fit in, gave her the space to often be the leader, particularly when it came to the social scene. 'But sometimes I felt like the pied piper.

There would always be lots of people around me, but on reflection I can see that the majority were only there for what they could get. Entry to a club or free tickets for this or that. I could make people laugh and generally ensured everyone had a good time. I provided a lot for the group.'

While people were drawn to her for fun and for what they could get, Sharon was often also drawn to the people who needed something. 'Birds with broken wings' as we deemed them in our conversation. She noticed them and felt their hurt deeply. She was the supporter of people; people in trouble, people in situations of domestic abuse, people who just needed to talk. She was there for everyone. It's no surprise really that she has spent most of her life working with people who have broken the law for some reason, she wants to give them a second chance - she wants to help them.

But when she needed people, when she needed a friend - the crowd had dispersed.

Sharon had attracted transient people to her. 'I just thought that friends come and go. I never felt there was anybody who was around forever. And that felt ok, I can make friends easily, with a lamp post if it will let me' she told me 'so I never worried about making new friends.' But in 2010 when she was diagnosed with breast cancer some of those friends drifted again. 'They struggled to talk about my illness, and I wasn't always much fun. I wasn't in the habit of asking things of my friends so even then I didn't really tell them what I needed.' Some drifted back when she was well, which she ensured was as quick as possible. 'I went back to work far too quickly and put on a brave face, it made others more comfortable and that was important to me.' she said, even then thinking about the comfort of others. I recognise this, sometimes I don't feel like telling people that I am sad or stressed or unwell because their reactions can feel like another thing to manage and look after. Keeping it to myself can at times feel like less work.

But in 2011 when the doctors recommended a hysterectomy to reduce the risk of spread, some of those friends disappeared altogether. She ploughed on - masking her needs even from herself.

When she returned to work for the second time however, there was a notable shift in one conversation that was going on. It was gradual at first but she leaned in to learn more and the conversation grew. 'I've never been a fan of labels' she told me 'so I hadn't taken much stock in ADHD and things like that when working with offenders, but we started talking about it differently. I started learning about it more.' Sharon told me how it had moved in her colleagues' minds from something talked about in passing or with cynicism to something real, something that may truly have been contributing to the challenges the offenders faced. As she learned more, she not only saw some of the offenders she worked with in it but 'I started seeing myself in it too.' Sharon recognised herself in the descriptions of ADHD, her childhood self, her teenage self and the grown woman she was now. She said that she felt seen in a way that she hadn't before. She'd always felt liked, but now she felt understood. So much so that in 2020 she went to the doctor and requested an ADHD assessment.

She reached the top of the waiting list four years later around the same time as her second breast cancer diagnosis in 2024. She went for the assessment and was told that she did in fact have ADHD. 'It was amazing,' she said. 'It was validating! I wanted to go back to people throughout my life and say I told you so! It helped me totally reframe how I saw myself. I realised there were certain things that I could do better than other people, there are certain things that I just had a gift for.' Sharon returned quickly to the confident, self assured child who justified her classroom behaviours because she was bored. That kid wasn't incapable of listening or missing something - she just needed more, because more was going on in her head.

'I love being ADHD!' she stated loudly 'It's everything, this is who I am.' She embraces it. She embraces the quirky way that her brain works compared to some others. She takes strength from knowing who she is, who she's always been and that it's not a disorder but just a brain that is running at 100 miles an hour. 'I bump into things all the time,' she said. 'My brain is just ahead of where my body is.'

I once saw a description that painted neurodiversity as an array of different operating systems - like Apple and Android. It's not a disorder, just different code. This short statement was key to me understanding neurodiversity and to looking at myself and how my brain appears to work differently to others.

Sharon had always appeared to have faith in herself to the outside world and that faith attracted people to her, but now she was tapping into it at a deeper level. It wasn't a mask of confidence but actual confidence. She loves who she is.

Getting to know herself more through her cancers, and then viewing herself through this new ADHD lens helped Sharon ask for help from people too, and do so in a way that truly served her. She described how her new found confidence had helped her to ask people not to cry in front of her when she was suffering. Instead she told them exactly what she needed and they did it. 'I fell down the stairs and broke some ribs not long after my surgery and when I called my friend to help I warned her 'I'm in a bit of a state and I don't need you getting emotional, I just need help.' and she came over and was incredible.'

The friendships that endured her illnesses and her ADHD awakening 'evolved so much over that time because of me showing, probably for the first time in my life, a great deal of vulnerability.'

'I have fewer friendships now' she went on 'But the ones I have are incredible. It's like we're family. It feels unconditional - I can be entirely myself with them. I don't have to mask anymore.'

She referenced our mutual friend who used to be a work colleague of hers 'She saw me at work, 'work Sharon'. But now I've shown her a different me, she's seen the real me. And she still likes me! She loves me! It's such a gift to be loved for who you really are.'

Sharon shared with me how she is still working on all of this. Having faith in herself despite thinking differently, despite doing things differently, despite all the messages of opposition to her that she's had in her life. Sharon has confidence in her right to be in reciprocal friendships, friendships in which she can give *and* receive.

In 1938, Harvard researchers embarked on a decades-long study to find out the secrets to happiness. The first thing to absorb here is that some people are predisposed to be happier and more upbeat than others, but what that doesn't mean is that some of us are incapable of increasing how happy we are. Quite the opposite. Wherever we are starting from, we can be happier. Aside from genetic predispositions, the research also suggests that about 40% of people's happiness comes from the choices we make.

The study itself, now in its eighth decade with some of the original participants in their nineties, has followed the lives of 724 men from a variety of economic and social backgrounds. Every two years the researchers collect all sorts of health information and ask the men about their lives, their mental health, and their emotional wellness. Over these eighty years, one of their key findings about being happy, which echoes the thoughts of Brené Brown and runs parallel with this book's exploration, is the need to be connected, the need to have close relationships.

Professor Robert Waldinger, the current director of the study and a professor of psychiatry at Harvard, contributed to a CNBC article by Marc Schulz, also an associate director on the happiness study. The article listed seven keystones of support needed in our relational lives:

1. Safety and security - who would you turn to in a crisis?

2. Learning and growth - who would you turn to for encouragement and belief?

3. Emotional closeness and confiding - who can you tell anything and everything to?

4. Identity affirmation and shared experience - who has been alongside you in moments that shaped you?

5. Romantic intimacy - perhaps we've covered this in the chapter on love?

6. Help (both informational and practical) - who is your problem solver?

7. Fun and relaxation - who lifts you, makes you feel connected and at ease?

This of course doesn't mean we need seven friends in our life, and those of us that don't need to go out on the hunt to make up the numbers, or that we need to cull a few and leave ourselves with this new magic number. These are not individuals but instead an observation of the needs we have in our social interactions. Needs to be met for optimum happiness.

What does strike me though is not just thinking about who I would turn to to meet these needs but who I provide them for. When am I someone's security or their cheerleader? When am I a safe place for vulnerability? How often do I remember to park the deep conversations that I am drawn to when someone actually needs to be relaxed and have fun?

If we go back even further than the start of this study, if we head all the way back to c. 350BC, we might learn a few more things about friendship that will guide our sense of the grown up ones. 'We consider a friend to be one of the greatest of all good things', writes Aristotle, who valued friendship above romantic relationships. He goes on: 'For no one would choose to live without friends but in possession of everything else that is good. Friends are of help to the young by protecting them from mistakes; to the elderly by looking after them and making up for their failing powers of action; to those in the prime of life, to help them in doing good things.' I love that his observations bring in a sense of the purpose of friendships. It meets my need to be of value in my relationships. I'm also not 100% sure that the friends I had in my adolescence protected me from mistakes - some got me into some big scrapes, but I probably did the same for them!

In his book the *Nicomachean Ethics*, Aristotle describes three 'species' of friendship:

- **The friendship of utility**
  These are the friendships that we form around a reason - we work together, we live next door to each other, our kids are at school together. These are the friendships that we enjoy through circumstance but will dissolve away quickly if the situation changes. When we change jobs, move house etc. While the name might suggest a transactional relationship, and it sort of is, it is no less valuable than other forms of friendship.

- **The friendship of pleasure**
  While utility revolves around mutual needs, the shared nature of it may not be something we love or choose. On the other hand, a friendship of pleasure is built around a common goal or interest. We play football together, drink together, and love the same music or books. And the friendships deepen with specificity. It's not just that we like to drink together but that we both like pubs with cider and a pool table rather than a bar with a dancefloor, for instance. These friendships can also dissolve but will only do so if the shared interest changes for one or other person.

- **The friendship of excellence (or virtue)**
  This refers to a friendship built on a love of the other just for who they are. We may have nothing notably in common, no shared sports or music or books, but our characters are drawn to one another. Aristotle himself said that this was a rare thing, but once found would be for life. Or as Michel de Montaigne puts it, 'Our souls mingle and blend with each other so completely that they efface the seam that joined them, and cannot find it again.'

To put these three friendship types another way, and to quote the poem by Brian A. "Drew" Chalker, People come into our lives for 'a reason, a season, or a lifetime'.

What the first two types of friendships have made me realise is that I have tried too hard sometimes to hold on to friendships that were ready to dissolve. There was no sadness or nastiness, we hadn't fallen out, the friendship didn't fail – it had just served its time, the reason or season had passed. The thing that brought us together, the shared interest or practice has changed for one or either of us. But when I haven't been able to maintain the friendship I have been wracked with guilt for having let it fade.

And perhaps the final version of friendship is the one I have in the friend who visited me when I was pregnant - it relaxes me to believe this. I don't need to be of value to her. I don't need to have common likes and dislikes. Perhaps our 'souls have mingled' and now there is no seam or reason - and there doesn't need to be. That's a lovely thought.

What this summary from over two thousand years ago has helped me to see is that even with the people who I once felt so close with, it is ok for us to move on if we no longer have one of the above types of friendships. There are a few that I am now ready to let go of. I want the best for those people, but I am now, metaphorically, waving them off into the world. Not because I don't want them around me, but because I no longer feel the need to 'maintain' the friendship. Instead I can let the two of us drift apart naturally and with warm feelings toward each other. And it feels wonderful.

A friend of mine that hasn't yet drifted and I were chatting recently about the pressure of social media and particularly instant messaging platforms. You send a message and can see when someone has read it. You can even see when they are typing back. The perceived ease and convenience of it makes it even easier to fall into the trap of trying to stay in touch and maintain a friendship that has run its course. That's not to say that there are people I wish I never heard from again. Not needing to hang out with them as much as I once did doesn't mean I don't want to hear about their lives, it doesn't mean I don't hope that they will be happy and actually, now I think about it, it also doesn't mean I wouldn't rush to their house to be there for them if they needed me. I care for them, that hasn't changed. If they need me to meet one of their seven needs occasionally then I'll be there. But let's not schedule a weekly coffee when we no longer have anything to talk about.

I think what I have also navigated poorly (and this goes back to my lack of confidence in my friendships) is when a friendship has moved from one state to another. My colleagues are a great example. On the face of it they are utility friendships, we spend time together because we work together. But as I neared the due date of my second child I noticed that I started to feel lonely in anticipation of not seeing them. Why would they want to see or speak to me when we aren't working together during my maternity. I was experiencing a friendship of pleasure, even excellence, but I didn't for a second consider they would be too. During one emotional meeting I blurted it all out - I was pretty hormonal of course. But I was met with surprised looks. They thought we were friends too - 'real friends'. I saw them often after I had the baby, Woody, and now consciously refer to them as my friends rather than my colleagues – because they are!

I do have other friends with whom I share an unconditional bond. An old school friend recently sent me this text after months of postponements and delays to a meet up - 'I'm so glad we can cancel on each other.' And I remember smiling and relaxing as I read it. We can cancel on each other because we understand each other, we know the other is busy, we know life is busy, and we know we want to be together at some point. If we didn't have all of that understanding and trust we would probably meet up when we said we would, we would put ourselves under undue pressure rather than risk falling out or breaking up our friendship. We usually see each other once a year for twenty-four hours in a spa hotel somewhere. We talk non-stop, we eat, we swim, we sleep, and we hug goodbye. We know we may not text again for months and we know that messages may go unanswered for weeks at a time. But we love each other, which means we can take the risk, be vulnerable and cancel on each other - safely.

An attribute of healthy and grown up friendships that I feel is beginning to crop up in this research is vulnerability - a need to be seen and heard without judgement. And perhaps the level or context of vulnerability may change depending on the friendship type but it's there. Grown ups feel safe in their friendships.

This makes me think of an unsafe friendship when I was younger. A friendship with a person who would play people off against each other in such a jovial and well practiced way that we rarely stood up to it. To stand up to it would have appeared petty. Instead we rolled with the bad days and hoped that we would be the chosen one next time we met. It was unpredictable, confusing and hurtful; and I know the group wore bruises from it for a number of years afterwards.

Looking back, it wasn't a friendship for that person or me - there was no vulnerability, there was no safety. It was an abusive relationship. But it was the relationship of young people. Humans whose bodies and brains were still developing. Humans who hadn't yet made sense of the relationships in their lives leading up to that point. Humans who were desperate to be included.

Twenty years on, I feel for that person. I think that poor teenager was fearful of something, protecting themselves from being seen for some reason, likely riddled with insecurities - like the rest of us - and found their security in controlling those around them. I hope that person now has friendships of excellence in their life. I hope they feel connected and seen by someone in a way that allows them to be vulnerable. I hope they are safe enough to let someone else lead.

Sarah's story

Sarah spoke to me from her home in Hanoi at 10pm her time - we'd never spoken before but given we were talking about making friends the whole thing felt pretty easy.

Sarah grew up in a small university town in Connecticut with her mum and stepfather while her Dad lived in Boston and later New York. Her parent's divorce was so amicable, and the sides of the family all so close, that Sarah said she didn't realise until much later in life that divorces could be messy and unhappy. 'It felt like just a widening of the family rather than a breaking of it.' She spent time in her town with her school friends and at least once a month would hang out with her Dad in exciting cities doing exciting things. She said that both her parents would introduce her to new and interesting people all the time, so she grew up with a wide variety of experiences.

'I had my long term friends in town but I always knew that life was so different everywhere else. I always felt different because I was exposed to many more things than other people from a very young age. I remember being eight years old and watching Joseph and the Amazing Technicolor Dreamcoat and just going 'Papa that boy is so pretty, I just like him so much' and he just said 'Not for you darling, not for you.' That's how I learnt about homosexuality. I had access to lots of things that made me feel different but it was my choice to be different. It never felt like it was imposed on me, I just felt I was very much myself.' Moving in and out of groups of people developed Sarah's ability to create connections quickly 'I would always find my people.'

After university Sarah and her Dutch husband moved to Egypt where she found herself socially at a loose end. This was Sarah's first time living abroad, but she took to it as she always had. She found a way into something that interested her and then invited others in, safely.

Creating friendships and communities and taking the potential challenges of languages and cultures in her stride.

Later they moved to Hanoi where they have been living now for twenty years. 'Moving to Vietnam was much more difficult' she told me, in Egypt her work had created her community but in Vietnam she didn't have that, yet. 'It was pre-internet, so I joined the PTA of my kids' school as a way to meet people.' The first few years Sarah noticed that her connections were made off the back of others inviting her in. 'When you live in an international community people sort of adopt you. Random conversations led to playing in a basketball team, or a running club, a knitting club, a cooking group, or heading out on a hike with people I barely knew.' Sarah developed good friends but in communities like hers people move countries or cities after a few years. 'You cannot survive in the international world without friends, and after a few years of people inviting me in I realised it was time that I started doing the outreach and inviting others. So now it seemed Sarah had two strategies.

The first was to greet people when they arrived in Hanoi from overseas and help them settle. 'When people arrive they are often not the best version of themselves. They have just moved a long way, it's all new, maybe it's not where they want to be or they haven't figured things out yet. But I have compassion for them, I will help them settle and then see who they are. I don't write people off immediately. So if I am nice to everybody then it benefits them and I find my people faster - it's both selfish and giving at the same time.'

The second strategy is when she actively rebuilds 'her team'. 'There was one year when I realised that a lot of my close friends had moved away, and I didn't really have any good friends here anymore. So I decided to have a rebuilding year - like a sports team does. I would go to more parties than I wanted to go to, do things I didn't want to do, and create the communities that I wanted to be a part of.'

This struck me as a very active and conscious building of connections and I admired it. It can be easy to assume that everyone is all set and you just need to find your way into their circles - I love that Sarah did that while also creating more circles. 'And you have to think about how you are - If I go into a PTA meeting and cross my arms then that's the energy I give out. But if I go in open and welcoming then I will attract people toward me. People will come and sit with me.'

In order to make people feel safe Sarah learnt that she had to be vulnerable - but after a lifetime of being herself and showing that freely and easily to others, it didn't feel scary to her. With a wealth of friends near her in Hanoi and now around the world Sarah tends to the ones that fuel her - but she's on the move again.

Sarah and her husband are soon relocating to be closer to their three children who are all studying around Europe. And again - she seems ready to create her new communities. But there is some learning to be done first. The other thing that Sarah spoke to me of in terms of making friends, alongside being herself of course, was recognising other people and what they need.

She recently completed her Dutch diploma in order to become a citizen alongside her husband - and there was a test. 'It was a cultural test really. Question upon question to ensure people understand the Dutch approach to freedom of expression and inclusion. But even after all these years with a Dutchman, there were two particular questions that I really learned something from and will come in so handy when I am trying to make friends in the Netherlands.'

The first question asked her 'if I have a problem with my electrics or my water then what should I do first?' In the UK we would probably assume that we should call the electric or the water company, and Sarah agreed that would be the first step in the US or in Hanoi. But in the Netherlands the required answer was that 'I shouldn't call the company first. I should try to fix the problem myself and then speak to my neighbours.' This may sound like a small difference but if you were living in an area where people ask each other for help and support as a matter of course, but when you have a problem you don't ask them, you may miss an opportunity to connect with your neighbours. Or worse you may send them a signal that says you don't trust them or want their help. You are literally not showing them vulnerability when they expect it. This was such an interesting example, a moment that could seem so 'everyday'.

The other question asked Sarah 'If you were visiting your new Dutch friends and you're having a good time on a Saturday afternoon and it's getting toward dinnertime do you expect to stay?' Again Sarah and I smiled and assumed that the party would continue in some way. But the answer is 'absolutely not unless you've made an appointment.' I was shocked - this is so different to how I live my life and how I am with my friends. There is of course no judgement in that - it's also wonderful to have the clarity of a finish time when you are socialising - but this is another tiny example where a cultural difference could trip us up and miss our window for connection. Sarah's experience of noticing that someone may not be at their best immediately after moving, inviting them into activities that may interest them, or learning the small social norms of a new country feel so important in setting ourselves up for friendship success! Recognising that they, and we, are vulnerable as we move toward each other.

'I give everybody the benefit of the doubt' she told me 'I try not to judge them or write them off, I think about what might be going on for them and what they might need, and what's going on for me and what I need - and some of these people become fantastic friends, and some don't - it works for me.' Sarah told me that the only risk in putting herself out there time and time again was that 'sometimes you meet an arsehole' but that it's a risk worth taking.

As we wrapped up our call, we chatted about how easy the conversation had been, how we'd exchanged stories, shared sad moments and laughed. I wondered if we were becoming friends...

Wow, she was good!

One night, while I was pondering grown up friendships my partner Jim texted me that dinner would be five minutes. I was sitting at my desk, and he was in the kitchen listening to a podcast about conspiracies as he made lasagne for us. I came down a few minutes later to find him texting - again!

Jim and a group of friends communicate constantly on a Whatsapp group, lovingly referred to as 'Ladz Bantz'. It drives me mad. It is a 24/7 stream of abusive messages and memes. He is never so happy as when four of them have piled onto the fifth's insecurity, failure or misjudgement. From the outside it could appear cruel, and I often tut when he shares some of the stories with me, unless he is the victim in which case both he and I revel in his downfall! But there is something underneath the 'bantz', there is something in this small group of blokes in their forties that allows them to, in his words, 'call each other the most obscene names in the morning and then be utterly vulnerable at lunch'.

As I wolfed down my salad in order to better focus on the lasagne, I asked him questions about male friendships. We talked about people we knew, and people we knew of. We talked of the stereotypical male friendships you see on TV and this common idea that men don't and can't share with one another. I asked him what it is that the members of 'Ladz Bantz' do differently to those who don't feel they can talk about how they are feeling.

'We talk about how we are feeling' he said, matter of factly and shovelled in a fork full of food. 'We do it with humour and in a safe space, but we get deep. Maybe not as a full group often but we will all, at different but fairly regular times, be in conversation with others about how we are feeling, how we are experiencing the world.'

I asked him if he felt there was a difference between men's friendships and women's - this was moving from a midweek dinner to an interrogation. His first response was: 'No, I have the same micky-taking-relationships with my female friends as I do with the lads.' He went on to clarify that 'of course' in a female-to-male friendship the question of 'sex' needs to be put to bed first - pardon the pun. 'But once you're both clear that there is no sexual attraction it's the same, gender is irrelevant. But what you really do need is a match in your understanding of nuance and humour - whatever the level, it probably doesn't matter, but you have to match.'

Then he reflected on some differences that did seem to exist: Jim thought that women seem to have a quantity of friends that men don't, but he wondered if men and women define friends in the same way. 'Women seem to call acquaintances friends. While I have people I will see for lunch, have a laugh with. But are we friends? - I'm not sure?' I wondered if what he was describing was the difference between utility friends and pleasure friends, as Aristotle might define them. And it made me wonder if women are quicker to name utility friends than men. And if so – why?

He went on to say that he probably has about ten people in his life that he could call in a crisis and know that they would be there for him - 'these are friends, despite not having seen some of them for years.' And that he has about five or six quality friends that he speaks to fairly regularly. 'But not all the time,' he added. I felt myself roll my eyes and I considered how many times a day I see him staring into his phone desperately trying to think of a put down to 'win' the bantz. I let it go.

This small group differed from the male friendships he had as a teen, he hastened to point out - where quantity was key! 'But now, who's got the time, or the energy? I'm happy to make new friends (ish)' he said, 'but I want depth and nuance. I want to be understood - and be taken the piss out of in a way that reinforces our friendship and our safety in it.'

We chatted and ate, and ate and chatted, and I pondered what he had said.

I reflected on another friendship I have with an old school friend. He and I can go months without speaking and then I will happen to be on a long car journey alone at the same time that he is waiting for a flight or similar and we'll talk for hours. But this is barely a catch up. We aren't enquiring into each other's spouses or kids - we go through the obligatory motions but we both know we are ticking boxes and we move on quickly. We speak about the world, about our worlds, about our feelings, our histories. And I realised as I thought of these conversations, and others that I have with a select few people, these are the conversations that fuel me. These are the conversations that I feel seen and connected in. These are the conversations and the friendships I don't want to dissolve. Not the exchanging of updates (although to be clear I do want to know about my friends lives and talk about mine occasionally) but the exchanging of stories, of experiences, of changing perceptions, of moments of clarity and of moments of doubt - that's what I want. I want to know who my friends are - not exchange newsletters with them periodically!

What was interesting to me was that the Ladz Bantz whatsapp group was a constant exchange of messages and abuse - but very little news. It was all connection.

So what strikes me is that while there may be 'species' and types of friendships, there are no set templates for the way a grown up friendship works - no set processes or systems. You may speak once a year or text ten times a day, you may make small talk and never leave enough time to really bare all, or you may walk in and cry without words.

Friendships, like the people in them, are unique - but what runs throughout them, what constitutes the thread of a grown up friendship, be it any of Aristotle's types, is vulnerability. Only when we are vulnerable with each other, and that vulnerability is received with gratitude, care and respect, can we feel safe in our friendships.

As I considered safety, my mind was drawn to my work. So often I am having conversations about psychological safety with my clients. An environment or relationship in which people can share ideas, ask questions, own up to mistakes, and, crucially, take risks without fear of negative consequences or judgement. I was then reminded of a team I worked with a few years ago - a team of friends who I think demonstrate what we're learning beautifully.

* * * * *

I was having one-to-one calls with each member of a technical department in a business I was working with. Our work often starts in this way. It gives us a great opportunity to build trust with individuals, get a feel for them and understand their perspectives. On this occasion I was speaking with them prior to them coming together for two days to work on their performance as a team and as individuals.

I sat in my office chatting with them through my laptop. As I clicked 'leave' at the end of the first conversation I remember feeling uplifted by the interviewees' joyous description of the team. They were incredibly supportive of each other, they helped each other out, they asked for help. In her view they were a fantastic team, built on years and years of friendship. The second and third conversations felt the same.

As I nudged them with questions about how they fed back to each other, how they challenged each other's work or how they disagreed, every single member of the team looked puzzled. 'Well, we don't,' they would all say, usually followed by a reassuring description of how close they all were, how they were friends. Something fishy was going on here. Everybody disagrees sometimes.

When the group came together in person and we began to discuss their performance as a team the conversations fizzled out. Eyes lowered to the floor, hands fiddled in their laps, and awkward, uncomfortable and nervous smiles or laughs flitted across faces sporadically.

This group had never disagreed with each other. They wouldn't dare. The risk was too high. They valued the friendships with the people they sat next to and worked with five days a week. They couldn't possibly chance falling out with one another. Instead, they bottled up frustrations, all ran their own individual processes, had little moans about each other behind backs, and never rocked this rock-solid friendship boat. And at the same time never trusted each other, or their friendships, enough to withstand a disagreement.

When the feedback finally started it was like floodgates had opened. Waves and waves of pent-up frustrations spilled out into the room and submerged the group in pain and negativity. In that moment, as tears rolled heavily down cheeks and expectations were sliced through with sharp comments, they all wished the gates had stayed shut. They all wanted to push the water back up stream, and pretend that it had never happened. They could return to what they knew, smile at one another, make playful small talk and feel secure in their team. But, the gates were open - there was no going back.

With support and time, their conversations slowed, lightened and became cathartic. The group became united in their relief at having spoken their minds. Yes, there were issues to be discussed in more detail, but as they realised that their friendships had wobbled and yet not broken, as they saw the hardship it took for others to say what they were really thinking, they allowed themselves to laugh at the absurdity of the years leading up to that point. Despite thinking they had these incredibly trusting friendships; they hadn't trusted the strength of them enough to ever be vulnerable and test them.

They tested them with us, and they survived!

In terms of grown up friendships I felt I was learning how important vulnerability was - showing yourself to others but also in taking risks and putting yourself out there, telling people what you need and hoping someone steps up. I noticed my growing comfort with the different types of friendships and how my anxiety over some of my friendships was itself dissolving. But this story about the team of friends sparked another question. Working relationships can be unpredictable and tricky to navigate. There are so many aspects at play. So I decided to follow our question of what it is to be a grown up into the workplace.

INTERLUDE

Resisting my urges

This part of my exploration has probably been one of the hardest. One of the reasons is that so much of my personal identity is tied to my work, tied to the work that I do and the clients and colleagues I surround myself with. My work is my hobby - I love it and I'm good at it.

This feeds a second reason that I have found 'grown ups in the workplace' a tricky thing to ponder, and it's that I have some very clear views of it already. In some ways it is my work. In fact I am coming to this chapter so clear on what I think the answers will be that I am struggling to be curious, struggling to truly switch on my 'learner', my explorer, and instead have an overwhelming desire just to tell.

The extreme irony here is that, in my work, I advocate for people to experience something in order to learn about it, rather than them being told about it in isolation. In fact I would never walk into a room of clients who have, for instance, commissioned me to support them in their leadership development, and tell them what a great leader is. I wholeheartedly believe that we learn and develop best by finding our own answers, by making our own connections. I want every reader of this book to finish it with their utterly unique take on what it is to be a grown up because each and every person has connected with, or been provoked by, a unique pattern of bits and pieces throughout the book - from the stories of others, from the research, from my ponderings and from their own reflections after they have closed the pages.

And yet - despite this tightly held belief, despite having built a career around the idea that it is exploration that leads to enlightenment - I find the ego driven part of me wanting to quickly give you the answers, and look clever in this chapter. My inner critic tells me that if I saunter into this chapter holding questions I will undermine my professional credibility. My heart tells me that if I don't I will undermine my everything.

So I saunter on...

CHAPTER 9

Working 9 to 5

What's the most grown up thing you've ever done or been a part of?

'I think being a Firefighter and the responsibility that comes with the title. I have to have my big girl pants on all the time, be ready for anything, and keep calm and do what I've been trained to do regardless of the situation.

There are times where your natural instinct is to do one thing, but your training is to do something else. Recognising it's that way for a reason and has come from someone else's knowledge and experience is key, taking it as an opportunity for learning and development, and accepting that I don't know it all - far from it!'

Survey respondent

If I am truly to explore this question, and not fake it while drawing on my preformed ideas and the theories of thinkers I respect, I need to do what I have practiced before. I need to visit my own experiences first and see where they take me.

The first workplace that I can actually remember is a bakery that my mum worked in when I was probably about six years old. Dad would often take us to pick her up and if we were there early we might go in and help her and the women she worked with close up. They would laugh together and enjoy themselves while they worked. I would often be given twenty pence from the tip jar for helping to clear tables - I loved the fleeting moments when I was part of their team, the remaining customers nodding and smiling at me as I took their tea cups. Work seemed like so much fun!

One of my mum's family-famous sayings when we were doing jobs or chores around the house was 'let's make a game of it'. She would challenge us to pick up all the toys in record time, or race to pair up socks. When we moved house we rode big books down the stairs like a slide before packing them up at the bottom. Rushed steamed puddings in the microwave were often bright pink with food colouring and accompanied by green custard, and leftover rolls from the bakery were the balls for short cricket matches that fed the birds - the bat of course being a stale french stick. We would roll our eyes at her enthusiasm, all the while enjoying the fun she brought to the most mundane of activities. She has always looked for the play, or the fun, in everyday stuff and I try to do the same.

I don't really remember my dad being in the fire brigade, although he was for most of his working life. He joined up by accident actually - he found himself at the end of a queue on Southwark bridge having just lost a job and 19 years later he was station officer at Shooters Hill Fire Station in Greater London. Sadly he was injured when I was about four and had to retire from active duty - he missed it sorely but his stories were joyous. Stories full of laughter and fun. Not the fires, of course, but the friendships, the pranks, the camaraderie. As kids we wore his old helmets and jackets when we had bonfires and I have a very hazy memory of once being dropped as a toddler down a fireman's pole by one guy and caught at the bottom by my dad - Dad says I have invented this memory and that he would never have dropped a toddler 15 feet, but I chose to ignore his loyalty to the facts and instead treasure the 'memory'. Yet again - work was fun!

I have another memory though, of around the same time, when mum was in the bakery, and it seeded something different in me. It felt at odds with what I expected of the workplaces that grown ups attended. It was a memory of bullying. I remember overhearing my mum crying with my dad about a woman at the bakery who was bullying her, being cruel to her, making her look bad, setting her up for failure. It was horrible to hear my mum being so sad, I remember feeling protective of her. But more than anything I felt confused. I didn't think grown ups bullied each other. Where was the head grown up to make them stop? Why weren't they in trouble? Didn't my mum, as a grown up herself, have the power to just say no?

Now that I am reflecting, I think these very early exposures to work probably formed two fairly deep seated beliefs in me that I am loyal to today - my tenets perhaps.

- The first is that you can have fun while you work, and still the work gets done. It's simple, but many of the most profound things are!

- The second is that bullying has no place in work. Bullying is in fact the opposite of grown upness, it is immature and, at its core, sad for all involved.

Sometimes beliefs can be so tightly held by someone that they become fact. This is how I feel about these two tenets. These are so indisputable to me that when I encounter the opposite, particularly people consciously driving for the opposite, I am as confused again as the six-year-old who overheard her mum.

Why would someone actively try to remove fun from a workplace?

Why would someone think that fun, while the work gets done, is a bad thing?

But some do.

Why would someone bully and be mean to someone else?

Why can't someone just say 'stop' or 'no'?

But it happens, and they don't.

Now of course I can name many reasons that these situations may crop up. I can picture the insecure colleague who wants power over others. I can hear the serious tone of the boss who believes laughter detracts from productivity. I have read the emails that purposely confuse or undermine for a reflective glow of rightness. I know the people, the good and well intended people, who are just a product of the system and have never thought to challenge the idea that dictatorship is synonymous with leadership. But despite all of this - I can never justify it. The scales never tilt in the favour of bullying. The scales never tilt away from fun while the work gets done. There is never a good enough reason.

I think these beliefs have been challenged many times throughout my career, sometimes by me as I have found my own way, but I have always come back to them. I have always wanted to find fun and have people find it with me. Are these the beliefs of a grown up though?

It might be easier, initially at least, to think about what a grown up in the workplace does not look like. A few faces pop into my mind's eye. Two faces pretty prominently in fact. I can see their painted smiles and their overly pressed suits. I can still feel the pangs of rejection as they dropped me from the great heights they had lifted me to, seemingly for their own entertainment. Playing with a young Sammy like a mouse. Deciding, on their terms and their timelines, when fun in work was appropriate and when it was something to be stamped out. Both had an overly inflated sense of their own intelligence, their expertise, their magnetism, their importance and their influence. Both thought they ruled the world, neither ruled very much at all. Both led with fear and intimidation. Both retold history so that they shone in it - and did so with such confidence that I was guilty at times of doubting my own memories. Both relied heavily on hierarchy as a structure to support them, and actually both were incredibly sexist, classist and disparaging of any kind of difference. They pitted people against each other, and created division in order to seemingly stop comradery forming in the ranks.

Both also made it hard to leave. They convinced me I was lucky to have a job. They took credit for my growth, my development, my successes - 'you were frying eggs when I met you' I was told by one of them, referring to my earlier roles in hospitality, as if he had lifted me out of an egg frying gutter and made me who I was. But they were both equally quick to blame if anything should go wrong - taking little to no responsibility for themselves and their actions. These were shitty bosses.

I encountered them five years apart in different industries and different parts of the country - but they were so alike. And they would have hated each other had they ever met, I can imagine them both slating the other for their behaviours - failing to see their reflection. I learnt a lot from them.

I had no respect for them whatsoever, despite feeling controlled by them, and at times I even pitied them. When not spun around by their behaviours but in moments of calm and confidence, I saw them as sad and insecure people. And I knew I wanted to be nothing like them. Not only because they weren't nearly as successful as they told themselves they were - and I wanted to win at the grown up game remember - but also because, behind the paper-thin facade, they were tragic - and that felt a far cry from winning too. Now I feel more sorry for them than ever. Now I hope they have found security enough to be nice, or not be arseholes at the very least.

The reason I feel like this about them is probably down to another belief, another tenet that I carry with me. It is that, ignoring genuine psychopaths and narcissists, I don't believe anyone, at their core, wants to get up every day and hurt other people or make their lives a misery. I just don't believe it. So I lean on this belief as I forgive them and wish them well - while hoping never to come into contact with them again.

I'm sure most of us have our 'work colleague horror stories', and they may be a good source of 'how not to be' and even a source of absurd entertainment - but can we learn what it *is* to be a grown up from them? Or from the bruises they inflicted? Perhaps, but let's lean to the positives for a moment instead. Let's see what we can learn from inspiring people, people who make us feel safe and supported in our work.

I decided to speak to someone I knew had made a fairly big shift thanks to a workplace event. I wondered what we might learn from his experiences.

Wayne's story

Our childhood has so much to do with the person we are later in life. Good or bad, it can shape how we see the world and how we see ourselves in it. It may shape what we need in our relationships and what feels unnecessary to us. My parents were both incredibly hard workers - they were always doing a chore or two. It might not take a rocket scientist therefore to notice the connection I have made between my value and my productivity. I was known for a long time as 'Sammy who gets stuff done' and I took pride in that. Even now, as I described in my friendships, I can struggle to see why anyone would want me around if I am not 'doing something'. I have really worked on this and it is a far quieter need in me and my work - but it crops up occasionally. Others may define their value in their expertise, some their experience, some their kindness, some by the power they wield. The really lucky amongst us may not feel the need to define their value through any lens at all - they are valuable simply because they exist.

In the workplace we can often experience these different definitions of value, and the different needs we each have. The different ways we each want to be led, recognised and appreciated. The different ways we respond to directness, support or challenge. And yet most leaders and most organisations have a one-size-fits-all approach to supporting its people. The outcome is organisations of people who likely fit into one of three camps: those for whom the one-size does fit; those who feel unrecognised whatever they do; and those who have redefined their value in order to fit. You can often notice those in the third camp because they are so different outside of work, in their mindsets, their personal values, their behaviours, their choices, their communities.

I have spent a lot of my life looking for a sense of approval, and when I chatted to Wayne I saw similarities in how he described his need for validation - albeit with a slightly different flavour and a potentially different origin. Wayne described feeling as though the approval, acceptance and validation of others, particularly people he saw as superior to him, shaped, in part, his view of himself – and how he presented himself. And it got him a long way in some respects, and held him back in others.

Wayne is the Chief Operating Office at a Global FinTech company, he has two beautiful daughters at home, is a husband to his childhood sweetheart, is a child bereavement counsellor - and a genuinely nice bloke. We met when his company became my client, and together we embarked on a programme to create a greater sense of belonging across a somewhat divided culture - not toxic, but showing some cracks of separation. He struck me as a man constantly in conversation with himself. A man who would have an allergic reaction to anything he deemed to be unfair or unjust - deeply feeling and supportive of the people around him. And at the same time a man who, in order to truly understand and act on someone's feelings, needed evidence to back up or justify their point of view. This tension creates inner conflict for him at times, a conflict he is tuned into and monitoring constantly.

In our work together I could see that he wanted to 'be there' for the people around him, and at the same time his logical brain was clambering to find answers to the experiences they described at work. But Wayne's desire to help others, or in his words 'to be the key', allows him to hold his inner tension, and use it to both support others and move forward with them. He agreed to have a conversation with me about grown ups at work, but our conversation started with a time way before he was in the workplace.

Wayne's story started when he moved from primary school to secondary school aged eleven. 'That's actually when my parents got divorced,' he shared. Parents separating is not an uncommon occurrence and Wayne was quick to dial down any sense that he was being dramatic: 'it happens a lot' he said. And he's right. My mum divorced her first husband with whom she had two children, my older brother and sister, then married my dad (his third marriage), having me and my younger brother. 'But it was slightly unusual for us in that we went and lived with my dad.' Wayne paused for a moment 'which, in the UK, doesn't happen unless, unless your mum doesn't want you.' He didn't pause after this statement – not even for a beat. 'So, I dealt with a lot of rejection and a lot of abandonment feelings,' he rounded off matter-of-factly.

My heart went out to a 10-year-old Wayne as his older self recounted the thoughts of the child. Whether his mum 'wanted him' or not is not something he or I decided to challenge. It was clearly what he thought at the time, and later he described how he had struggled to convince himself of any other possibility. While, as a mum myself, I wanted to rescue him and reassure him, I noticed that I stayed quiet. It wasn't my place, and he wasn't looking to be rescued.

He spoke theoretically about himself in the third person of how he was just a kid, a good kid, and that that kid had done nothing wrong - his mum wasn't leaving him. But he is self-aware enough to know that theory and logic doesn't always go far enough to counter deeply held beliefs. He grew up with his dad, a wonderful and supportive man, but also a little old school. 'If you got 99 out of 100 on a test he's the sort of man who would ask what happened to the one you got wrong.' Wayne told me, smiling.

'It wouldn't take Freud to surmise that my childhood might have something to do with the need for validation I experienced for most of my life,' He said to me frankly 'a need to be recognised and appreciated.' These needs aren't all necessarily bad of course, and they've driven him to achieve some amazing things. Given my similar need to be valuable I also wonder if, at times, it has been as exhausting for him as it's been for me.

'But I'm not sitting here relentlessly seeking an answer to that validation question," Wayne explained, 'I'm actually quite comfortable that I'll probably be on my deathbed and will have never fully resolved it. And I think sometimes that's okay.' Rather than play therapist with him, I wondered instead what we can learn from the impact of needing to feel valid, or the search for validation. How these needs impact how we are as grown ups, and how that plays out in the workplace - given employment is, in its most simplistic of terms, an exchange of value between two parties.

Wayne described how he found his validation in adolescence in various places; playing for the sports teams, being a welcome friend in a tight knit group of girls, being trusted with their secrets, being confided in, and having teachers not only praise him but invest their time and energy in him. He cantered through descriptions of how his friend groups and sports teams were together, and recounted stories to me that I then pictured in my own school field and playground. It sounded like a colourful mix of energies and inputs. All the while it sounded like Wayne was being himself - different aspects of himself - but himself none-the-less.

At school maths, engineering and logical subjects came easily to him, he would do well in those subjects without really putting any significant effort in: 'And the things that just didn't interest me or didn't grab my attention, like music or art or religious education I just wouldn't put any effort into at all. But the other part of school, that kind of 'belonging' bit, I struggled a bit more with that I think.'

As well as being an achiever in education, Wayne worked hard outside of school for his dad who had a variety of businesses, one of which was a potato merchant. "I passed my driving test with just five lessons because it was crucial that I got out in the pickup truck and delivered potatoes. I would go out some days when I didn't have college classes and deliver twenty or thirty tons! I think it instilled a real sense of work ethic in me.' In addition to the work ethic and sense of contribution to the home - he got paid! 'My dad was always quite fair minded. I'd get paid £0.10 per bag of potatoes so I could sometimes make £100 in a day!' Again I recognised myself in Wayne. I often worked all weekend in a pub waitressing when I was at school and college, taking on any babysitting or extra odds and sods that were offered. It was so satisfying to do something, have someone be pleased, and get paid for it. In fact for me it was a little addictive. I suspect it was this desire to be so demonstratively productive that led to me dropping out of college at seventeen to work full time.

Again like me, at a fairly young age Wayne was in lots of adult environments - be it when he played golf competitions in the men's category, when he was delivering potatoes to venues and restaurants, or when he was working the bar in a local pub. Even at University, his accountancy course was one that attracted mature students rather than teenage freshers. I wondered if he, perhaps subconsciously, felt the need to present himself as mature in those environments too - as older than his years.

His first 'corporate' job came from a conversation in the pub actually, and his second followed quickly on from a connection he made in the first. Wayne impressed people and moved up and around quickly. His maths acumen, his logical, problem-solving abilities and his incredible work ethic made him an attractive asset in the tech companies around him. 'I was the 'Problem Solver', and I had built my own value on being the guy that could be dropped into a problem (typically a project) and get it back on track.' I suspect that being the problem solver was hugely rewarding for Wayne. Satisfying his desire to be accepted and validating him and what he does - perhaps he felt like a grown up? I wonder if he was as consumed by this feeling as I was?

Wayne was being rewarded the way that most organisations reward their valuable people - with promotions, progression and money. He worked hard to meet others' expectations of him, and enjoyed the challenges he came up against every day. Challenges he could overcome.

He spoke to me very highly of the people he worked with, how they encouraged him and created opportunities for him, but at some point, and he wasn't sure when, he noticed he'd shifted. Rather than the team player he had been in his sports, behind the bar and in his very early career, he had started 'playing the game' in a different way. 'I'd built up in my own head a view of what was important to me. This was largely a combination of 'results and achievement'. Consequently, the trappings of being good at that were bonuses, promotions, salary, awards. I had also shifted to being far more tyrannical and dictatorial than I was comfortable with.' Wayne described how blame was thrown around the businesses he worked in. 'If these people weren't so crap, we wouldn't be in this mess' was the phrase I used often, and my managers validated my behaviour with 'Yes, thank goodness you're on it now Wayne, you'll fix it.'

'I felt part of the boys' club and accepted by my managers and leaders, because I was the solution.' I imagine at times this must have been very satisfying. Wayne isn't particularly comfortable receiving compliments but these behaviours will have circumnavigated the need to overtly tell him how great he was - the leaders inviting him in time and time again will have proven their need for him.

The celebrated behaviours Wayne demonstrated are often seen as part of a stereotype of the Alpha male in organisations - the quintessential leader. I've seen many people, men and women, overlooked because they didn't demonstrate this 'Alpha-ness'. And the organisations they were in were the lesser for it - lacking collaboration, accountability, empathy, safety, innovation and long term stability.

I tried to be an Alpha for a while. I dismissed those I didn't think were held in high regard by the people I wanted to be seen by. I distanced myself from the softly spoken or the introverts who contemplated and instead aligned myself with the 'impressive' and decisive extroverts who 'got stuff done'. This wasn't a long period in my career thankfully, it was a time when I lost my way, but I still look back on it sadly.

'It didn't make me happy.' Wayne continued 'I had the car, the house, the 'status things' of materiality that I thought I wanted, and yet I was pretty miserable.' I heard in him echoes of my grown up game. I wondered if he was inadvertently chasing what he thought he was supposed to want in life, what he thought success looked like, what he thought it was to be a grown up. I wondered if he'd started to see through it too.

Despite his misery, he was still subscribing to what he thought success looked like, doubling down on where he thought validation came from, so when a new opportunity came up in 2005 he and his wife couldn't refuse. It was an exciting move but one that required them to leave their home and roots in Saltburn and head South to Wokingham. Wayne's career progression continued without a hitch, and despite moving for a role as employee number one in an exciting tech start-up, he was shortly headhunted to a global giant - this was the big leagues! And it didn't take long for Wayne to be noticed there too.

'I was put forward, because of my 'ability', onto an intensive 'High Potential' personal development course called 'Stretch'. It sounded phenomenal and was run by some amazing facilitators.' Wayne told me. 'Five different one-week residential courses around the world throughout the year. It was made clear to us that this was a privilege to go on, as only 3% of the company ever got this chance.' I was excited for him as he described the course.

'And not just that, but of all the 'Stretch' courses held, very few of its participants went forward to the 'Boost' course,' the next level up so to speak. 'My mission was clear, I was going to win at Stretch, and secure a place on Boost. This would help me achieve even more promotions and material things to make me happy!' I smiled as Wayne flippantly described this. What an opportunity he was given. But the idea of 'winning' at a personal development course was laughable to both of us - and still, it was true. It's exactly the mindset I know I have taken to similar things in my life.

'I am going to win at this meditation class!'

'I am going to win at antenatal classes!'

'I'm going to win on this coaching course!'

I have even felt like it when I went on a singles activity holiday to Turkey on my own. A week of canoeing, kayaking, bike riding etc and I wanted to win - I wanted to be the most well-adjusted and least self-conscious single on the trip. I was not.

However we describe these markers of validation - for me 'grown upness', for Wayne 'winning' - it is a hugely powerful magnet to be drawn in by.

Wayne arrived early to week one of his course, 'ready to beat everyone with my intellect and my abilities.' He was ready for business! The type of business he was used to. The type of business where presentation, quick answers, expertise and an air of authority came out on top. However, business didn't seem to be on the agenda. 'I was utterly confused when the entire team of facilitators introduced themselves - they were all Clinical Psychologists. I remember thinking 'What the hell do they know about doing my job?'' Wayne prepared himself for disappointment.

At the end of a long and intense first day of self reflection and encouraged sharing, he sat at a bar with others from the course - confused. 'None of them were like me. None of them were there to beat me. None of them were looking to find fault in others to prove their own worth. They were asking questions of me and each other. They were naturally curious about each other.' He screwed up his face as if he were describing aliens.

'That first night was the first time I had ever felt outside my comfort zone. I called my wife from my room and unloaded on her about how I wasn't sure what to do, and I remember the wise words she said to this day. She said, 'Just be yourself, let them in, what have you got to lose?'' She was right - what did he have to lose? It was clear he wasn't going to win playing his well practiced role, and creating a new character was a risky business at this stage, so being himself was the only option. 'I decided to take a leap of faith there and then. I decided that whatever the outcome, I would do what I felt was right, not what I felt I should do to win.' In my imagination Wayne took off his grown up, professional, mask and let them see the real him.

'I didn't sleep much that night, but I awoke full of energy. I engaged the best way I could. I listened more than I'd ever listened before, because I wanted to hear what people said, not push my opinion to the top of the pile to win the discussion.' Wayne was practising something new, something he hadn't seen much of in leaders until meeting this group - it was risky, and he was enjoying the discomfort of it.

Something else curious happened too. 'The people I was working with asked me if I wouldn't mind presenting our work. They didn't want to have the 'spotlight' in front of the group.' Instead of seizing the opportunity to show everyone how clever he was, he noticed himself pushing it back to them 'why don't you do it, and I'll help you prepare for it if I can?' This was a total turn around on the Alpha who had arrived. This guy was lifting others up, and they appreciated it, and as a group they achieved more. And on top of all that communal 'winning', I found myself getting so much more satisfaction from watching more nervous colleagues stand up and do a great job, than I did from standing up myself.'

The first three days of the course were incredible. Wayne told me how he was so energised - he was alive with it. He was smashing eighteen-hour days and wanting more, more of these conversations, more vulnerability, more of these amazing people. And then...

At the end of the third day the facilitator set up the sessions for day four. 'Tomorrow we will go through the findings of the psychological tests' Wayne's heart sank. Prior to attending the course, there had been interviews, pre-work, and a bunch of 'tests'. 'The premise was that we would sit as a whole group, and each person's results would be put up on the screen, and we would look at how everyone's view of themselves was aligned to, or different from, the experiences of the group.'

The analysis had been completed before the course started, when Wayne was still doing what he could to win. 'I felt physically sick knowing that what was going to go on the screen was the 'view of myself' that I thought others wanted to see, I'd carefully answered the questions to result in the person I was well practiced at projecting into the world - not who I truly was.' Wayne had taken his disguise off and thrown it away, and now the whole group was about to discover it.

As Wayne spoke I too felt my heart sink. He was about to be found out. 'My imposter syndrome went into overdrive.' But how he dealt with it was a clear demonstration of the shifts he had made in just those first three days. Shifts not to someone new but back to who he really was. In these first three days he had found his validation, not from the facilitators' applause or their grades but in the acceptance of the group - in his unconditional sense of belonging.

'I spoke openly to the facilitator about it - telling them what I had done. He shocked me completely by putting his hand on my shoulder, and said 'Do you think I don't know this already." Wayne said he was confused; how could they possibly know? The facilitator continued, 'The person in this report is not the person we have met here this week.'

He didn't let me feel like a fraud for long, he simply said 'Why don't we take the tests again together, and I'll compile your true report tonight."

Wayne had one of the most impactful personal development experiences of his life. 'I ended up with two different reports, two different pictures of myself.' One was of the fake persona, trying to be what he thought 'business' wanted him to be. The other of the real Wayne. '100% authentic.'

'I was thirty-one at the time, and I often see that as the week that I changed my attitude. I stopped trying to 'win' and instead wanted to build teams that could win. I stopped wanting to be the best, and wanted to work with others and help develop them to be at their best.' He paused and smiled. 'Actually, I still try to win - but less so. I catch and moderate it much more. Wanting to win is part of my DNA, but I don't want to win alone or at the cost of others. I want to win *with* others.'

Wayne says that as a result of this experience he has become a better colleague, a more valued contributor, more certain of his own beliefs and values. 'And I was quickly promoted and recognised for my ability to build and bring together teams, and I stopped being seen as the person that would fix the problem, but instead the person who could ensure that the problems got fixed.' It's nuanced but it's an important difference - and one with much more scope for promotion ironically.

While Wayne told me his story I was drawn back to his need for validation and how it had morphed into a different desire for acceptance. Not by assimilation, to be accepted because he fit the mould, but a sense of acceptance because of who he was.

The Wayne that I met as a client two years prior to our conversation seemed such a far cry from the materialistic man who moved South in search of bonuses and promotions. The Wayne I have come to know is a man ready to challenge and ready to be challenged. A man obsessed with his own development, always carefully listening for an old voice in his head that might steer him in the wrong direction. A man who told me that the best day at work is one where someone asks him to help them achieve something themselves, 'particularly if they are seeking me out because someone else has recommended me - yeah that's ultimate validation.'

When I took stock of our conversations and reflected, what really stood out to me was less of what he said and more of how he spoke – it was deeply considered and utterly caring – and authentically him. His story made me think of a quote by Eric Berne: 'We are born princes and the civilizing process makes us frogs.' and reinforces my belief that the vast majority of people are good, we just get bent out of shape sometimes by what's around us - and what we think our surroundings require of us, turning us into frogs. There are plenty of frogs at work.

In my work, when I am around people like Wayne I often feel I am in the presence of grown ups but there is an irony to this. I don't feel like it because he has his shit together, or has all the answers. I don't feel it because he is leading the room or others appear subservient to him. No, it's his awareness of the qualities in him that don't serve him well - his awareness of the frog. He knows that he isn't perfect, that he isn't everything, that there is work to be done. And I can see him actively and openly doing that work. And more than that still - it is watching him work on himself, watching him get uncomfortable and yet push on, for the benefit of others as well as himself that cements my view that grown ups in the workplace are always working on the frog while trying to be the prince or princess - for themselves and for others.

There is so much research conducted on workplaces, on businesses, on leadership, on performance - and of course, as yet, none on what it means to be a grown up there (perhaps that's Book Two?). When I asked my survey respondents about being a grown up many of them mentioned work or getting a job. It was one of the highest recurring themes alongside 'Responsibility'. But in that sense it felt like it was one of the possessions of a grown up - 'I will have a job' - or a means to an end - 'I will work hard so that I can provide for my family.' Apart from the quote at the top of this chapter from a firefighter (not my Dad) none talked about what work needed from them, or how they needed to be. And yet the vast majority of research into what makes high performing organisations suggests that they emerge when colleagues are happy, fulfilled and connected to what they do or the colleagues around them - when we feel part of something.

Perhaps therefore we can look at high performing organisations as a lens on grown ups in the workplace. A study by André de Waal in the Netherlands tried to define a High Performing Organisation (HPO) and find a (practical) way to measure them. The researcher conducted 'an extensive systematic review of the literature on HPO' and from that created some themes and a resulting definition. At first glance, the answer seems fairly banal - it concludes that HPOs can be measured by their success when compared to their competitors. For all the reading they must have done this doesn't feel like a startling discovery. But when looking deeper, what was interesting was that 'success' wasn't a synonym for profit and wasn't determined by its customers; it was instead determined by the organisation's colleagues and managers. How the people that work in the organisation think and feel about it is its measure of success.

So what are people looking for in organisations that may result in them rating them as 'high performing'? Well a 2025 Gallup survey asked 13,085 employees in the United States what was most important to them when deciding whether to accept a new job offer. The highest scoring response was 'a significant increase in income or benefits' - 64% said this was 'very important'. This has always been a highly scoring answer in Gallup surveys, and perhaps unsurprising but Gallup did say that what surprised them was 'how much 'pay and benefits' have increased in importance.' Since 2015 this answer has risen from number four to number one.

I assume some of this is down to the cost of living increases around the world and the high employment levels, however I also wonder if there is something in this about stability. Perhaps people are looking for consistency and stability in a time of increasing uncertainty, so effectively 'you'd have to offer me a lot of money to make it worth the risk of moving jobs.'

Number two on the list was 'Greater work-life balance and better personal wellbeing,' which was backed up by other recent surveys that tracked the increase in work-related stress and burnout, or the fear of these. Our awareness of burnout and our resistance to undue stress appears to have changed over the past decade. A move to hybrid working has allowed people to see what is possible, imagine another way of operating in their lives with some positive and some negative impacts. While many people love working from home and being able to pop the washing on between calls or walk the dog at lunch, others find they are working longer hours and don't have a clear and clean line between where work stops and home begins.

The third desire of prospective employees when considering a job offer was 'the ability to do what they do best'. Gallup found that 'workers who aren't allowed to use their strengths very often seek jobs where they can; workers who do get to use their strengths seek out jobs where they get to use them even more.' We want to be utilised, we want to be useful, we want to be stretched and to grow without being burned out.

One desire that surprised me came in at number five with 43% of people saying it was a key factor in their decision. It was that the organisation has 'Covid-19 vaccination policies that align with my beliefs'. This comes after some shifts in US legislation around people in certain positions needing to be vaccinated, and found that people felt incredibly strongly on both sides of the argument - that it should be mandated and that it shouldn't. We could surmise that this is simply down to the view of their safety but I think there is something deeper here. Layer this on to the shifts in the States recently on the conversation of DEI and we start to see that employees want to know where their employers stand politically. They want organisations to have a view on things and not sit on the fence.

I recently became aware of an organisation that presents itself as incredibly progressive, climate positive and, in essence, liberal. People join because they want to be part of a movement, and people buy their products for the same reason, wearing the brand like a badge to indicate their views of the world. I was made aware that the owners had chosen to fly from the UK to the US to attend the inauguration of Donald Trump. Whether you are a fan or not you can see the incongruence here - and so could they. Their attendance was kept a secret from their employees, for fear of repercussions. The view was that if people knew they 'would have walk outs on their hands.' So whether we are leaning left, right or wobbling in the middle politically it seems there is a growing desire to be part of an organisation that, at the very least, takes a position too. There has always been a link between business and politics, although historically it has been convenient to pretend there isn't, but now, with the increased public awareness of political impact on them in a very real sense, organisations are being forced to suck it up and tell us how they feel.

In my experience and in the conversations I have had researching this question of grown ups in the workplace, people do want to know where their colleagues stand on topics - not necessarily political topics, but decisions from 'the top' or opinions on changes. They are unsettled by the 'company man' persona that always toes the line. In a focus group recently the colleagues agreed that when pay increases were paused due to a tricky financial situation they would have rather the CEO said 'and this is shit. I feel terrible and I'm sorry' as opposed to the emotionless way the facts were stated. 'It felt inauthentic. It was shit and it would have been great to hear her say it - at least then we'd feel like she was with us.' I can picture this situation, I've seen it many times. The CEO or leader behind the scenes acknowledges that what they are about to say is awful, and they are suffering from it too. But it is unavoidable and understandable. Instead of saying that however, they slip on a professional mask and distance themselves from the reality of it, believing that to be reassuring and proper. I wonder therefore if when we experience grown ups in the workplace we feel that they are not wearing a mask at all, and like Wayne, they are their real selves, they are human.

*****

In all organisations there is usually, not always but more often than not, a Parent-Child relationship at play amongst the people. Maybe not with everyone, maybe not in every department, but nine times out of ten - it's there. Lots of frogs had by the system.

The phrase parent-child comes from a theory by Eric Berne in the 1950s called Transactional Analysis. It is a psychological theory developed from Freudian psychoanalysis and focuses on increasing our awareness of how we are responding in an interaction (or transaction). Berne suggests that we are each made up of three 'ego states' and that we move in and out of each of these parts all of the time. The first part is the Parent - which in itself is divided into two, the controlling parent and the nurturing parent. How we enact this parent will be led by the behaviours of our own parents or parental figures. And both types of parents have positive and negative outcomes. The controlling parent may stipulate clear boundaries in order to keep us safe, but this can go too far and they may become authoritarian, scolding and directive. The nurturing parent may be caring and loving, but they could become smothering, protective and overbearing.

In the workplace it is easy for people to slip into these roles. The stereotype of good leaders can often lead to the controlling parent who takes charge, telling people how and what to do. I've also experienced many leaders who lead with their nurturing parent and protect their teams from failure or feedback, stunting their growth and development. And these roles aren't limited to leaders of course - we can all slip into these roles. When travelling with a colleague I often take charge of the logistics until one day she told me that it can be a little condescending when I navigate her around the tube. I had never imagined it that way - I thought I was being helpful.

The second 'ego state' is the Child - which, like the parent, is divided into two, the adaptive child and the free child. Like the parent state, our behaviours or beliefs when we enact our child will be largely guided by how we were as a child. The adaptive child will adapt to social situations, using their 'internalised social learnings' to be what will be accepted or needed. For example 'I know that apologising when I did something wrong fixes the situation because it always has before'. A person who got their way by sulking as a child may result in an adult who, when in their adaptive child state, will sulk. The free child however can appear to be all win - they can be creative, spontaneous and playful but when overplayed they can have little to no social constraints and not observe any social or expected norms such as saying thank you when handed a coffee or adhering to speed limits on the road - the rules don't apply to them.

What is fascinating is when you start to think about the Parent and Child together, interacting. The controlling parent scolds and by way of response the adaptive child apologises. The adaptive child sulks and the nurturing parent gives in. The free child pushes boundaries and the controlling parent puts up more boundaries. In the workplace these are easy traps to fall into - mostly because we are fairly well programmed to respond in the way we have been addressed. If I am spoken to like a child, I am likely to respond as one. These are known as complementary transactions - we essentially meet each other's expectations of us. And this can continue forever. Berne said that 'So long as transactions remain complementary, communication can proceed indefinitely.'

But what if it doesn't? What if, when spoken to as a naughty child I respond as a controlling parent too. 'How dare you speak to me like that?' Where will that push the other person to? They may back down immediately and move to their adaptive child and 'I win' - this will reinforce my confidence in these behaviours, I made them change. I will then probably repeat that behaviour again and again 'indefinitely'.

But wait - there is hope! There is a third ego state - the Adult. While the parent and child draw on life experience and influences to characterise themselves and drive their behaviours, the adult is in the moment - in the here and now. They use all of their abilities to stay in the moment and treat the other person as an adult too.

It is amazing to me how many leaders I have seen hire someone for their experience and expertise and then, on day one, tell them what to do. They hire them for their potential to be awesome and then parent them like a child. Timekeeping systems that require us to clock in are parenting us, and how do some people respond? As the free child trying to get one over on the system. Others revert to the adaptive child and don't leave when they are ill for fear of repercussions. If we tell someone in our parenting voice that we don't trust them, then they will behave like people who aren't trusted. But if we speak to adults as adults - or let's say 'grown ups' - well now it gets exciting! If we say to someone 'I hired you because you are right for this job and I trust you to get the job done' the chances are that you will have the potential of an incredible colleague on your hands. On my first day in a role as an account manager the MD gave me a credit card of my own. I didn't have to earn his trust - he gave it freely and hoped I didn't abuse it. And I did not.

For the majority of my career I have worked in agencies or as a consultant. This has given me the opportunity to experience hundreds of organisations, and thousands of people in their places of work. I've worked with manufacturers and charities, tech giants and cushion makers, financial services companies and aeronautical engineers. I've worked with professors and students, with stage performers and counsellors, with lawyers and ecowarriors. I have had deep and meaningful conversations with farmers and people with life limiting diseases, comforted CEOs of global brands and calmed the nerves of finance directors and chefs. I have been blown away by the unexpected and comforted by the repeating patterns. I am so grateful for the breadth of interactions I have had so far, and find it a source of constant growth and development for me - how could it not be right? And in all of these organisations, I can honestly say that Adults succeed. Like Berne's Adult, grown ups in the workplace are in the here and now 'drawing on all of their abilities' for the current context and treat the people around them like grown ups too, and they do so as themselves, authentically showing up time and time again.

* * * * *

I recently headed to another cafe in Bath, this time to meet Sienna - the daughter of my business partner. I had asked to interview her because it felt to me she may be at an intriguing moment in her life at which to consider what it is to be a grown up. Sienna was nineteen and just rounding off her gap year before she headed off to Cardiff University to study English and Psychology. She's an intelligent woman with an exciting future ahead.

Looking back now I realise that I was hoping for an interview about the fears of 'having to grow up' at uni. Worries about fending for herself, cooking, shopping and so on. But that's not what Sienna gave me.

'I can cook, I like to cook so I'm not worried about that. And I'm going to be in really nice halls so that will be fine. And I've been working for the last year so if I have to get a job that will be fine too.' She seemed entirely unfazed by all the things I had expected her to be holding nervously. Of course I was pleased for her, I don't want someone to worry, but I noticed myself feeling a little lost in my interview with her. Where might this go then?

Meandering satisfyingly around subjects of friendships, love, school and work I enjoyed the difference in our generations. The conversations of inequality, climate change, procreation, that she was having with friends was a far cry from the ones I had had at that age. But I know I would have loved to - perhaps I didn't have the confidence to instigate them?

Then, as we pondered on her future and what it may look like she said something that surprised me. 'I just don't think it's healthy, all this home working and remote working. I want to go to an office'. This goes against everything you hear in the media and the pressure we are putting on a move to hybrid working where we can work both from an office and from home.

Sienna finished her coffee and told me that when you are at school there are people you don't get on with but because you have to go to school you have to see them. And when you're older and you have to go to work there are bound to be people you don't like too. People you don't agree with, whose views you don't share. We discussed how you might have to sit next to someone with a completely different political view to you and at times their view of how the world should work is bound to be apparent - as is yours. Sienna's worry is that if we aren't forced into situations, like offices, where we have to spend time with people different to us we will only spend time with the people we choose. And those people are likely to be people like us.

Social media has also given us a huge amount of choice over the voices and opinions we hear and those we don't, which is why some of the more recent political decisions have been so shocking to one side or other. When I woke up and found we as a country had voted to leave the EU I couldn't have been more shocked. Everyone I spoke to, everyone in my little echo chamber, was voting remain. Who were these millions of people who had voted to leave? I didn't know any of them - or so I thought.

The levels of division that we are experiencing all over the world and the moves to extreme right and extreme left is likely to continue if we keep choosing to only associate with people like us, this I had considered before, but Sienna's point around offices was a new factor I hadn't clocked. In environments that we don't get to choose, our biases and beliefs are more likely to be challenged at times, we may learn something about a topic or perspective we had written off - we may find a connection. When we are alongside people the same as us the outcomes are potentially more predictable but when we are with people who are different... Well that gets exciting!

Maybe we should go back to the office - to meet with strangers - for the good of society!?!

From here I felt reassured in what we had learnt about grown ups at work - that they are vulnerable, respectful, self reflective and treat others as grown ups too. But I wondered what it meant about strangers? What can we learn about what it is to be a grown up from our relationships with strangers?

CHAPTER 10

Strangers in the night

When did you notice a grown up not acting like a grown up?

'When my Dad shouted at the woman in the post office and it wasn't her fault'

Survey respondent, 10 years old

While scrolling mindlessly on Facebook recently I was stopped abruptly by a black and white image of a woman with a detached look on her face, staring into space. The article was titled 'Would you let strangers do whatever they want to you?'

I began to read about the Grandmother of Performance Art, Marina Abramović, and her 1974 experiment in a gallery in Serbia. Surrounded by seventy-two objects of 'pleasure or pain', including pens, lipsticks, feathers, olive oil, a scalpel and a pistol with a bullet, Marina stood still for six hours, only giving visitors guidance through a small sign that read 'I am the object. During this period I take full responsibility.' She wanted to understand what strangers might do to another person if repercussions were removed entirely.

Initially, people were hesitant to use the 'pain' objects and instead handed her flowers, kissed her gently or sprayed her with perfume. Over time, however, visitors began to test her a little. Approaching her with weapons to see if she might flinch or resist. When it became clear that she wouldn't, the objects and their potential became more attractive. Within three hours her clothes had been cut off of her body, her stomach pierced with rose thorns, her body sliced with the scalpel and a wound made to her neck and drunk from by visitors emulating vampires. Her face was drawn on and her humanity lost.

Eventually a loaded gun was held to her head and the experiment was called to a close. Surrounded by two groups of strangers, the first, her protectors arguing for her safety, and the second the inflictors of pain arguing for their right to do as they pleased, Marina left crying, bleeding and naked. Humiliated and violated by fellow humans just because they had the freedom to. 'After exactly six hours, as planned, I got up and started walking towards the public. Everyone ran away, escaping from a real confrontation.' When her statue-like state was broken and people were reminded that she was a living, breathing, feeling person they were faced with what they had done, and they fled. 'What I learned,' she writes, 'was that if you leave it up to the audience, they can kill you.'

This story really troubled me. It challenges one of my beliefs that all people are, at their core, good. That we don't want to inflict pain on one another but instead if we had free rein we would look for ways to please and pleasure one another.

I can of course understand the thrill and attractiveness of a set of societal rules being removed, like the appeal of smiling at someone on the underground, having dessert before the main course, or a ménage à trois - my free child living their best life. Though none of these actions are particularly drastic, they all carry with them a small sense of rule breaking, and with it potentially a sense of exhilaration. But I cannot imagine approaching someone with a gun and holding it to their head, just because they told me I could. I cannot imagine cutting someone's skin and drinking their blood just because they took responsibility for my actions.

It reminded me of the famous Stanford Prison Experiment in 1971, a social psychology study funded by the US Office of Naval Research in which volunteer university students were randomly assigned the roles of prisoners or guards in a simulated prison environment. Initially, as you'd expect, the roles were held lightly and playfully; however, it didn't take long for the guards' sense of power to cloud their judgement and they became more and more authoritarian. On just day two the prisoners rebelled and the guards cracked down further.

The level of abuse and mistreatment by participants against their peers playing prisoners was so drastic, in fact, that the experiment was stopped after just six days. Some guards became tyrannical while prisoners were traumatised and disorientated. The experiment has been widely criticised over the years and isn't a fair test of the average human condition - but it is worrying.

Do these two examples tell us that people can be cruel to each other, or did they both simply attract the types of people who want to push boundaries or have a sense of power? Who knows? And does this tell us much about grown ups? I'm not sure about that either. But perhaps it's a helpful reminder that as humans, we can still be animals with animalistic desires and instincts.

What it does tell us in our search for grown upness though is that when we dehumanise somebody we lose empathy for them. In both examples the artist and the prisoner were no longer Marina and 'Greg' - they didn't have names, they had objective nouns and numbers. They weren't people any longer. I see people, one after another, walk by a homeless man on the bridge by the train station in Bath. Avoiding eye contact so as not to acknowledge his humanity. Pretending they don't notice him, hoping he and others will forgive them their uncharitable behaviour. When speaking with homeless people during a piece of work years ago I was told that the hardest part is 'having your humanity stripped away'. One man told me that he can go days without someone truly looking at him, that he feels invisible most of the time. A ghost wandering the high street. A smile or a nod would have gone a long way.

In situations where we are frustrated in the face of a process or a seemingly faceless brand it can become easy to forget that the individual we are speaking with is not that brand: the woman working at the post office is not The Post Office. When I asked a group of ten-year-old children what grown ups do that isn't very grown up, one answered 'When my Dad shouted at the woman in the Post Office and it wasn't even her fault.' I cringed. Recently, an inconvenience on board a ferry owned by a multi million pound company led me to aim my frustrations at the people wearing their logo. Rather than hold my irritation and voice it through a complaints line at a later date, I unloaded onto a woman at the information desk, a woman with zero control over the situation or its outcomes. What a shitty thing to do. Thankfully, I took a breath and recognised what I was doing. I recalibrated, returned to my adult state, apologised and worked hard to reassure her that I was aware that she was not personally responsible. But there was a moment when to me she was no longer 'Camille' but instead 'the brand.' I dehumanised her, giving myself permission to berate her.

I suspect we do this a lot in everyday life, be it hanging up on the cold caller who is just trying to make a living or deeming another driver to be 'an arsehole' by way of excusing our anger toward them. In these cases we create no space to think of the other as a person too - who may be having a bad day. I wonder if we do it to protect ourselves.

A few years ago when Jim and I were both flat out with work and kids we employed a cleaner once a week to keep our house from falling into utter filth. They were lovely people, two women running a small cleaning business, hard working and super friendly. Despite their friendliness, I hated being home when they came. I hated interacting with them.

It wasn't because of them, or who they were but because if I didn't see them as people I didn't have the same sense of embarrassment about the state of the house, I didn't have to watch them enter a dirty bathroom or open a disorganised fridge, I didn't have to hear what I imagined would be horror when they saw the state of the lounge or the piles of dirty washing donning the landing. I could just come home and imagine that the house magically became clean while I was out. I did, however, check in with them, asking them if the way we left the house for them was ok, did it meet their expectations, and so on - I was looking for some forgiveness and acceptance I think. They always said 'we've seen worse' - and rather than dig into this I would text back something like 'Lol Phew!' and shyly move on with my life.

*****

This idea of dehumanising strangers also makes me wonder about times when I have been the victim of it myself. When I was seventeen I worked in the restaurant of a holiday camp on the South Coast. 'Restaurant' is generous, it was the bar in which microwaved food was served to hungry families and holiday makers. It was far too small for the number of people the site attracted at high season and could be an incredibly stressful environment for everyone at times.

On the bar we would take order after order as fast as we could, detaching ourselves from the poor guys in the kitchen whose printer would be spewing out all of these demands. We passed the buck and we did it fast. Then, on the busy nights when people returned to the bar angry and frustrated at the wait time for their food, the buck was promptly passed back to us and we had to try and calm them. No one in those situations saw any other party as human, but instead as another amorphous being causing frustration or harm to them.

One evening, when the bar was particularly busy, three or four people deep, I stood at the food till in my uncomfortable bright orange shirt trying desperately to keep up with demand. While I took the order of a happy holiday maker who was relieved to have finally got to the front of the queue, a man pushed his way through the crowd, plate in hand. His face was red, his eyes narrow and his manner incredibly aggressive. The sound of the arcade, the music and the bright lights made the moment loud and intense. On the plate was a pie, a pile of mash and some gravy. Instinctively, the person I was serving and I both stopped and looked at him. He screamed at me that he had waited ages for his food and then it had come out cold. He assaulted me with a tirade of judgements and insults. I tried my hardest to apologise and offer solutions - holding back my emotions. The people around him at the bar, clearly shocked by his behaviour, stayed quiet, giving him an audience and an even greater sense of power. Eventually he stuck his index and middle finger into the pie - time slowed down for me as I watched him - and, in order to prove that it was cold, flicked its filling at my face. I'll say it again, I was seventeen. This didn't hurt me physically - it didn't burn me, obviously, as the pie was stone cold - but I felt violated. I felt humiliated. I felt attacked. I felt entirely unseen by him. There wasn't an ounce of empathy in him. He didn't see me as a person but as the 'process' that had resulted in a terrible evening for him and his family.

Perhaps dehumanising someone, or creating distance between ourselves and them, removing a sense of connection to them allows us to shed our responsibilities, our sense of what's acceptable. Think trolls online protected by their anonymity.

Splattered in gravy I took a deep breath, saw the shock in the faces of other customers and stepped into the back room to call the manager on duty. That night the security manager was in charge, a massive bloke who was not to be messed with. I told him what had happened and he stormed around to the restaurant from the camp office. He took the money out of the till, threw it at the man and told him to 'fuck off'. Probably not the best customer service, and not what I wanted to happen, but he too dehumanised the guy. He saw him not as a man on holiday with his family who had sat for an hour with hungry kids only to receive cold food, but instead as an object to be removed.

That entire situation was one of division. When I got home that night I finally exhaled the breath I had held all evening and sobbed.

So if it is the absence of connection that allows us to treat each other terribly, as 'ungrown ups', then why is it that some people treat others so beautifully, putting themselves at risk for a total stranger's well-being when there is no apparent connection in place either?

Kay's story

Kay couldn't remember how her realisation came about, maybe it was a newspaper article or something on television, perhaps it just popped into her head without a catalyst - however it happened, Kay said she suddenly realised that donors of organs didn't have to be blood relations - they could be utter strangers.

In my search for forms of, what I now know is called altruistic biological donations, I came across the charity Give a Kidney. I popped in an email and within minutes the CEO Jan replied. We arranged a video call and talked broadly about donation and why people do it. 'You need to speak to Kay,' she told me. 'I'll introduce you.' I am now starting to believe that Bath, where I live, may be the centre of the universe as despite Jan living up North and the charity being based all over the UK, Kay had moved to Bath a year prior. We exchanged emails, had a quick call and arranged to meet in the cafe of a local garden center.

When I arrived at the cafe I walked up some steps and saw a woman sitting on the first table I came to, she looked welcoming and didn't look away when I caught her gaze 'Kay?' I asked and she beamed at me, inviting me to sit down. We shared a little small talk, niceties really, before ordering teas and pastries - there's a theme emerging here!

We began chatting easily and Kay took me back to 2001. 'I had always thought that people could only donate to blood relatives because of the connection, that it was a genetic thing. And then I realised that no, husbands and wives do it too. And even friends do! And I thought, well, if that's the case, there's no reason why somebody who didn't know somebody else couldn't donate.' Kay made it all sound so obvious and matter of fact - and it was really. She told me that she didn't know what sparked the thought but once it was there she couldn't shake it. 'So I wrote to the Minister of Health and said that I would like to give a kidney to someone who needs it.'

She received a letter back telling her that she was not the first to offer her kidney to anyone who is a suitable match but that there are two big issues that make it impossible. The first is that the law states doctors cannot do anything to someone 'that is not in their best interests', that is, to give away a kidney that is serving your body well. This has been circumnavigated with donors who are spouses or friends when they have deemed that the donor will benefit from the recipient's health improving. The second reason is a fear that someone is being paid, coerced, or forced to donate. The letter told her that the ministry of health were working on this and the government were considering changes but it all sounded a very long way off. The letter told her that a storyline in a recent soap about someone needing a kidney had garnered a few similar letters, but no - 'you can't do it'.

Kay shied away from sounding like she was doing anything particularly altruistic at this point and simply described herself as a terrier who couldn't let go. 'If someone tells me no, I just keep on pushing,' she told me.

Subsequent letters back and forth dug further into the risk of exploitation but Kay felt incensed. 'But there was no comparison because, you know, they spoke to me about money changing hands. And I wrote back and said, 'but I know nothing about the person! It's far less likely that money could possibly change hands if the agreement is through a government system than somebody who asks their neighbour down the road.'. She told me that at this point she did go a little quiet: 'I was worried they'd have me down as a lunatic!'

Her letters led to her views as a member of the public being included on a paper lobbying for changes to the law, it took a while and was complicated by a few scandals around 'unlawful donations' but in 2004 the The Human Tissue Act was passed. Kay was told that should she still want to, she could begin the process of donating her kidney to a 'suitable match'. The law to actually donate however didn't come into being until September 2006.

Being the first meant it wasn't clear sailing from then on, however: 'it was like the Wild West because they had no sort of protocol for it.' There were no systems set up to handle this, no procedures to follow or experiences to draw upon. The whole thing was handled by the Royal Free Hospital which meant regular trips from her home in Hertfordshire to London, sometimes to meet with consultants who weren't exactly sure why she was there or to have tests and the testers weren't available. At one point, when she thought things were moving along nicely she was told that to give the donation she would need to first see a psychiatrist, someone to deem her sane.

The hiccup was that the waiting list of a psychiatrist was nine months, another delay. The Royal Free decided to fund a private session and so Kay travelled yet again for another appointment, this time to prove she wasn't crazy.

'Years later,' she told me as we poured more tea and she ate her danish far more slowly than I had mine, 'I was approached by a doctor at a convention where I spoke about kidney donation. He told me that he still thought I was crazy.' I laughed as she said this, assuming the man was good humoured in his comment. 'Oh no,' she continued, 'he really thought I was crazy! It's Catch 22,' she said, 'an impossible situation - you'd have to be crazy to want to donate, but if you're crazy they won't let you!'

The psychiatrist however hadn't thought her crazy and had given the ok for the donation. More paperwork, more tests but the end was in sight and a recipient had been identified 'a perfect match apparently.'

All Kay knew was that the recipient was a woman who lived in the North of England and needed a kidney. This is where I started to struggle a little. While I wanted to feel as content with that minimal information as Kay was, I found myself itching to know more. For a moment I felt protective of Kay - 'would this person look after her kidney?' As I shared my discomfort with her she laughed: 'and this is why I believe anonymous donations make much more sense than giving to family or friends,' she said. 'When you give a kidney or whatever to a sibling or a child or a neighbour you don't have to see a psychiatrist, no one prepares you for the emotional challenges you may face in the future watching that person walk around living their life. If they don't look after themselves, or stop taking the anti-rejection medication as some do, you are there - still in relationship with them. Imagine how bitter you could get or upset, imagine how it could impact your mental health and your relationships. Giving to a stranger means that I have very little knowledge of what's happening and therefore I can choose to believe that that person is living their life however they want to and I may have helped them live that life for a little longer.'

I could see her logic and why perhaps when a husband or wife isn't a match but a donor can be found that may well be a good thing: 'often anonymous donors are people paying it forward - they couldn't give to someone they wanted to so they want to put a kidney back in the system by way of exchange - it's beautiful really.' I wondered if I would be strong enough to watch someone I loved abuse their body if it had my kidney in it. I would like to think that I could but I have a strong suspicion I'd find it hard at best.

The whole process took from August 2006 to July 2007 but when Kay arrived at the hospital the night before her surgery she was still met with bewildered looks. 'So you're donating to him?' the nurse asked, pointing to her son.

‘No’ Kay answered.

‘So he’s donating to you?’ the nurse asked.

‘No, I’m donating to someone in Sheffield who I don’t know.’

Quick yet quiet conversations were had between the nurse and the doctor on call after which the consultant approached Kay and her son and asked ‘and have you arranged transport for your kidney?’

Now Kay was confused. She’d come this far, pushed the government, contributed to lobbying papers, challenged doctors, seen a psychiatrist, had God only knows how many tests and had multiple conversations with her four children all to be met by the same blank faces she always had been.

“Let’s go home,’ suggested her son but Kay’s terrier tenacity kicked in again.

‘No!,’ she said ‘the woman who needs my kidney will be checking in now too, she’s expecting it, she’s counting on it, I’m not going to let her down.’

It struck me that there were so many points in her story where Kay could have quit. And no one would have blamed her. She’d tried her hardest but it wasn’t going to happen, she could have gone home with her two kidneys and felt satisfied with her efforts - but she didn’t. She didn’t even entertain it!

‘We went out for dinner locally and returned later that evening and an empty bed was finally found in a random ward.” The surgery went off well on the whole but due to a minor complication it was a slightly different approach than they’d planned. ‘I felt for the surgeon really,’ Kay said. ‘It was supposed to be laparoscopic (minimal opening up), and I think he'd done about a hundred laparoscopically, but I had a tiny vessel that tore. And so I got a conventional incision.' Kay's kidney was whisked off on the back of a motorbike to its new home and she stayed in a few more days to recover.

Kay told me that when you donate a kidney they always take the smaller of the two, 'although some people have three!' But that your remaining kidney will grow in size to compensate. 'There's really no downside,' she told me happily.

As I found myself agreeing with her and mentally planning to donate one of mine my thoughts drifted to my sons - what if they needed one one day? Guilt of having given it to a stranger washed over me but Kay said that her children had asked her the same: 'what if one of us needs it?''There are four of you,' she told them, 'and if more and more people donate then should you need one, hopefully, you'll find a match but I shouldn't hang on to mine just in case.' She talked about how anyone needing a kidney is someone's child. They are someone's mother, father, sister or brother, they are someone's lover or friend. They are another human being in need - in need of something she had and didn't need.

Without a story, a face or a name Kay had, without any effort it seemed, humanised someone to the point that their need was more important than the potential needs of her children. It was incredible to me. I wondered about the connection she had formed with this faceless recipient, what she imagined about them, but again she seemed confused by my fascination. 'After 5 years I was curious and I asked how the recipient was doing and I was told she was well - so that's nice.'

Again I noticed a sense of ownership bubble up in me as I imagined myself in Kay's shoes. 'How is MY kidney doing?' I heard myself say but Kay smiled gently at me, as if to a child and said 'but it's not my kidney, it's hers.' I sat in awe of her, full of admiration and respect - not just for the act but for the 'grown up' way I experienced her to feel about it now. I quietly scolded myself for not being grown up enough to live and let live after my imaginary kidney donation.

To me she seemed extraordinary. I cooed over her, comparing her to the super humans that Jim and I experienced in midwives when we had our children: 'they're a different species,' he would say about them. But rather than flattered she appeared frustrated. 'When people say things like that I say to them that I don't think that I'm different or special. This is something you could do if you wanted to. If we're in good health and found to have two kidneys we can spare one.' She told me that the risk with seeing her as a superhuman is that it gives people a way of not truly considering it. 'But I'm an everyday person, and everybody is capable of this, you know? So go and do it if you want to.'

Her comments weren't with any judgement, quite the contrary actually. She said 'I don't think everyone should or could do everything. I'm not a strong swimmer and if someone were struggling in the water I probably wouldn't jump in because I don't think I could help. We should just do the things we can do.'

I started to smile, laughing at myself, as I realised the irony. I had been thinking about how she humanised these strangers, saw them as simply other people of equal value alongside her on this planet when I noticed that in order to distance myself from a pressure to do what she did, recognise that her altruistic act was within my grasp too I had dehumanised her - made her a 'different species.'

We took different routes out of the garden centre but then crossed paths again in the car park. I offered her a lift to wherever she was going but she told me the walk does her good. Moments later I drove past her striding up one of the longest and steepest hills in Bath and I thought 'she's only got one kidney - by choice.'

You don't need to donate a kidney to connect with strangers in a meaningful way. But if you ever need reassurance that strangers do the most wonderful things for each other then listen to the Radio 4 Saturday Live 'Thank yous' - a slot dedicated to strangers thanking strangers for incredible acts of kindness.

In one, a woman thanked a stranger on a train who listened, heard and comforted her on a tough journey between addiction treatment centres, accepting her without judgement. 'Fifteen years on, I'm living happy, sober and free in the real world, feeling able to look that world in the eye. [The woman on the train] really helped me so much with that.' The caller held back tears.

Others thank strangers who paid for their shopping, their train tickets, or rescued them when they broke down. People who looked after strangers' children in moments of crisis, invited families in during air raids in Iran. One man thanked a neighbour who was previously a stranger yet gave him a car when he noticed the family were struggling: 'that car allowed me to get back on my feet and turn my life around.'

I have been the stranger helped by another. I had my card declined once when shopping: there was nothing I could do about it. I felt embarrassed, but the person behind me at the checkout simply paid for my food. No drama, they just nonchalantly said something like 'we all have those days' and then moved on. I have been comforted when panicking on flights multiple times (I'm not a good flyer), have had my tyre changed by a passer-by when I had no idea where to start, and been invited in for tea after I broke down in tears when collecting something I had bought online.

I have tried to be the gracious or helpful stranger too. Not to be a hero, and not in order to tell a story about it, but because if that's how I want the world to work. If that's the world I want to live in, then I need to demonstrate it. And I would be lying if I said that it didn't feel good too. Doing something for someone else is a gift: it feels incredible to have been there for someone when they needed it, to have perhaps surprised them, to have left them with a renewed belief in human kindness.

The University of Sussex teamed up with Claudia Hammond and BBC Radio 4 to run the world's largest public study of kindness. The group received 60 thousand responses to their study asking about the last time someone had been kind to them. 'Ten percent of people said this most recent act of kindness had come from a stranger,' said study lead Dr Gillian Sandstrom in a blog of her experiences.

'People told us about strangers doing things like sharing an unexpired parking ticket or carrying heavy groceries to the car,' she writes, 'But they also told us about minimal social interactions: a smile, a compliment, a friendly chat. These are small, humanising acts that cost us little time but can be more meaningful than we realise. Indeed, research suggests that people underestimate how positively a compliment, a thank you, or an act of kindness will be received.'

The World Happiness Report lists countries in their order of happiness. One of the tests on it asks people to imagine they dropped their purse or wallet and consider how likely it was that someone would pick it up and return it. The report then carries out these tests, dropping wallets with money and contact information in them. These tests allow the researchers to measure the level of happiness, through trust and cohesion, of that country. A recent 'wallet drop' test in the UK saw all ten wallets dropped in Belfast returned with the money intact.

Would we deem an act of kindness toward a stranger as something that is grown up? I'm not sure. Would we class the act of dehumanising someone in order to treat them poorly as the opposite of grown up?

I suspect so. And if the difference between the two acts seems to be about finding a human connection with that person, seeing them as human, in order to be together with them in the moment, then perhaps the idea of connection is becoming even more important to our definition.

Lee's story

My social feeds recently seemed to be overwhelmed with the polarised reactions of a single news story. The Supreme Court ruled that the definition of a woman is based on biological sex, and that trans women with a gender recognition certificate (GRC) could potentially be excluded from single-sex spaces if 'proportionate'. This felt like a big deal to a lot of people. It didn't impact me directly and yet I felt aggrieved by the blunt and simplistic nature of the conversation and the outcome. Most contributions had been dumbed down to a point of uselessness - as often happens in politics, important nuance was ignored for the sake of quick adoption and entertainment.

I felt angry about the nuance that had been missed and the impact it would have - I noticed my lack of compassion for some of the lobbyists.

Then I saw a post on social media from a Trans Woman named Lee. It was written with such grace and calmness. Lee had stepped back from the emotions swirling around and instead applied compassion and understanding. She paused and reminded people of a few things; that trans people hadn't been stripped of their rights, that whether or not they have a GRC they are protected under the Equality Act, and that exclusion still needs to be justified. It was a calm grounding for many I suspect.

She went on to describe some views that she holds that differ from what many might expect of a trans person. She wondered where

Trans Men were in this conversation and worried for them being forgotten - potentially being asked to pee with the women. And how will that make the women feel? To have someone who is a man in appearance, behaviour and personal definition venturing into the changing rooms?

Her points were made with a quiet confidence in who she is, and compassion for the world she lives in. I had to speak with her. Thankfully she was up for it and by the end of the week we sat opposite one another, albeit via our cameras and screens.

I entered holding an assumption - a dangerous thing I have come to learn. I told Lee that I wanted to speak to her about her post, and understand how she accessed such empathy in the face of aggression. She smiled as I told her about the book and what I was trying to learn and nodded to some bits that clearly resonated. Then I said 'And I imagine you've had more need to be compassionate in your life than perhaps I have' and her face screwed up. Not in disgust but in disagreement. I had assumed that Lee had been a Trans Woman for a long time, and that therefore she would have faced the worst of society at times, that she would have been disrespected, dehumanised, excluded or abused in her life. But her story was not the one I pictured and I felt a little silly for my preconception.

'I knew I was trans when I was eight years old,' Lee started. 'But I didn't do anything about it until I was nearly 40.' By this point Lee had told me about her children, the youngest of which was 16 so I could tell she must have had children while she was living as a man. 'Our family is still together, my wife and I are very happy' she shared and I felt my heart swell. Millions of assumptions were now swirling around in my mind, but they were all loving and positive so I let them be.

Lee came out as trans 'and then almost immediately lockdown hit. And it was the most amazing time.' Lockdown gave Lee the time and space to really think about who she was. It gave her the space, without the eyes of the world on her, to begin transitioning, to explore what this meant for her and her family. It was a secluded time in which she could ready herself calmly to one day step out of her front door as her authentic self.

While I won't pretend we went through the same scale of change as a family, lockdown was a gift for us too. It gave us the space to work out how we wanted to be together - and to rework our lives to make that possible. Don't get me wrong Covid and Lockdown were awful for many many people, and neither Lee or I wanted to belittle this - but for us both it was a time to take breath, take stock and make meaningful changes.

Lee described the emotional and physical pain of her transition, but on the whole - 'it could have been a lot worse' she said. But she 'jumped off a cliff, knowing it was the right thing to do and that it was going to be scary and painful' but she did it with people around her that loved her - whoever she was. And from that she has found great strength.

'Where do you find your compassion for these strangers then' I asked, taking us back to her generous post 'in the face of conflict or hurt?'

She thought deeply for a moment and then shared with me that she thought there may be three types of compassion.

'Sometimes it's instinctive, it's tied to something you believe about the world or you have experienced.' I get this, it's easy to feel for someone who is being laughed at because at some time or other most of us have experienced that. It's an unconscious compassion.

'Then there are the times when you use compassion to solve conflict' It's a conscious decision to see the other person's perspective and to be curious about it. This is what Lee had done in the post that caught my eye. She had looked at the situation from a number of perspectives and held them all lightly. Sometimes we describe this as 'meeting people where they are'.

'Then there is the compassion that serves me' she said. Again she described a conscious decision to access compassion but this time it was as a mechanism to let things go. I smiled at this - I do it a lot. If someone cuts me up on the road while driving I have a choice. I can either get angry at them and carry that rage for the rest of the day, or I can assume the best of them and pour a bucket of love over the person running late, or on their way to the hospital, or who didn't understand the road layout. I can feel for the person who may be driving away feeling terrible for having accidentally cut me up. And I can forgive them and move on with my day. This serves me really well.

Our conversation ventured into complexity. 'The problem is' she continued, 'as human beings we want things to be binary. It would be so much easier if they were.' She then described the desire for things to also be linear and consequential 'If you are this then you do that, and if you are that then you do this, it's clear and predictable - but the world doesn't work like that'. We discussed how, despite a prevailing view that things are different now from how they used to be, the world has never really been that straight forward. But how most of us have bought into the convenience that things are binary, and turned a blind eye (at best) to anything that didn't fit.

But we've always had trans people, we've always had people with autism, we've always had homosexuality, we've always had single parents, biracial relationships, and every other type of person and way of being in the world. These are not new. What is new is the societal pressure to recognise, accept, celebrate and live alongside each other peacefully.

Jim and I aren't married - 100 years ago we'd be shunned in our little village. Our children deemed bastards and our non religious practices probably deemed the work of the devil. But times change.

What Lee and I were describing in this inconvenient truth was that things aren't binary - and yet people clambering for them to be actually holds us back as a society. If there are only ever two views, we will always be polarised. Judgement, hate and simplistic thinking will win.

'Compassion cannot exist in a binary world.' She said, I absorbed that statement deeply, and scribbled it down, circling it twice on my pad.

'Compassion cannot exist in a binary world.'

Perhaps part of being a grown up is accepting the uniqueness of each and every stranger, and being curious about them before we accept the certainty of our opinion.

It was winter, it had been raining all day and it was dark and gloomy already. I was starting to think no one might turn up for my experiment. I never worry about that when I initiate something. 'If no one turns up I'll have a glass of wine alone and go home.' That's what I told myself, and others, in the lead up. But now I was there, glass in hand, starting to feel a little nervous.

As we neared the start time people began to drift in out of the rain. Faces I knew who found me with a hug and faces I didn't who I identified by their quizzical looks around the bar. Drinks were purchased and we wandered up the stairs. Given the purpose of the evening I thought I had better start things off before people chatted too much and got to know each other. I took a deep breath and began. I welcomed the group of around 18 people to the very first gathering of 'Fascinating Strangers.'

One of my favourite things to do is to talk to strangers. Despite what my parents told me. I don't just mean to pass the time of day with them, discuss the weather or reside in a shallow exchange of polite facts - however valuable we may now know this to be. No, I like the deep stuff. I've had this around campfires at weddings and outside nightclubs in the smoking area when I was a lot younger. I had it once on a train that broke down. I've had it on holiday, in loos, at taxi ranks and even once on a blind date that wasn't going anywhere romantic but was a brilliant evening of fascinating debate. But my favourite place to meet strangers will always be at a house party - specifically in the kitchen!

The best way I can describe it is when you end up chatting to someone about super personal, incredibly important, or vastly theoretical topics in the kitchen at a party. Deep and meaningful stuff that has the two or three of you utterly captivated. Then, as you part for one reason or another, you turn and say 'oh, I'm Sammy by the way,' realising you'd skipped the formalities.

There is something weirdly freeing about the anonymity of being with strangers. There is no relationship in place to protect or worry about, certainly no 'catching up' to be done as you've never met before, and no commitment to become friends or take it further. It's just a moment of human connection in which you hear them, they hear you and then you part.

During Covid I missed these accidental interactions with people. Even if you did bump into strangers out walking everyone was mindful to keep a distance, or if a conversation was struck up it was about Covid, or the NHS, or something along those lines. By November 2022 I was ready for some kitchen conversations, but I had a three-year-old and a baby and wasn't going to that many parties. So I tried to recreate them.

I invited a handful of people who didn't really know each other, but knew me, to experiment with me. To see if, by avoiding introductions, avoiding job roles, how many kids, how was your journey here etc etc etc, and prompted by a single open question, we could create a space for meaningful conversations without any strings. I couldn't believe that people said yes.

Granted, on the face of it, this probably appeals more to the extroverts amongst us and sounds like an exhausting way to spend a winter evening to the introverts. But, some did come. They came more to support me than they were drawn by the idea, and one said 'if it was anyone else I would have said no because it sounds awful.' And yet she came.

I thought a few boundaries would be useful, but not too many, so I suggested we try the experiment for two hours with the following guidance:

- We talk to whoever we want, that may be the same person all night or everyone in the room. This is not networking so there is no need to fit everyone in.

- If a conversation feels like it has run its course then leave, move and join others.

- We all attempt to be as open as we can be, lean into the discomfort and trust that something will emerge.

And then I posed the question to kick us off: 'What is revealing itself to you right now?' A purposefully broad question that I had stolen from my colleague Graham who used it in a group session the week before. I stood there as the room continued to look at me and with a nervous laugh I said 'Well, go on then!' The group echoed me with similar awkward giggles and turned to each other. And it began.

During the evening I noticed a seventeen-year-old and a fifty-something talking about friendships, a group of four or so discussing divorce and separation. A pair seemed enthralled in their theoretical discussion about change. The climate crisis came up, love, loss and children too. I wandered into conversations about confidence, imposter syndrome and descriptions of inner critics - mine of course was hiding from the glow of the evening. People showed themselves to each other over and over. It was incredible to witness. Four hours later I had to break up the party. The pub was closing. There were handshakes and hugs as these fascinating strangers parted ways and I couldn't have been happier! It worked!

The next day I received emails from people still high on the experience of talking with people they didn't know so vulnerably about things that were so important to them. Someone who classes themselves as an introvert told me how freeing it was to be allowed to just listen if they wanted. And not to feel obliged to scan the room for their next conversation partner, under the pressure of 'meeting everyone' or 'networking'. One guy said that he had already told three people about it that morning and was enjoying regaling them with the magic of strangers.

That was a while ago now, and I haven't hosted the second one yet. Life has got in the way. But I will, when the time is right. What we created in that room above the pub was a safe environment. People had been invited by me or someone else that they trusted. They all had the same brief and clarity of expectations. They didn't know each other but they were now safely bound by something - connection. Similarly in the kitchens at parties or on the broken down train, there is something shared. We are in a crisis together, or we are enjoying something together, we have a trusted point of reference. We are no longer strangers because something bonds us.

Depressing though it is to consider what we can do to one another, what we are capable of, when we dehumanise it is hugely encouraging to think about what we do for strangers when we do find a connection - be it charitable giving, or a moment at a check out. Even when those people are thousands of miles away just trying to keep their families safe from the war around them we can sometimes find connection. We see another parent, another child, another human.

Perhaps what we can learn about grown ups through this lens of strangers is that grown ups don't see them as strangers. They may not know much about them yet, they may not ever. But they see them as other living and breathing human beings on the planet - of equal value to them.

So, at this point let's pause. We've thought about romance, love and marriage. We've delved into friendships. We have looked inward to how grown ups are with themselves. Popped to the office and have now considered how grown ups are with strangers. There seemed to be a gaping hole in my research. A hole I knew I had avoided. I looked at a scribble of a stickman on a notebook on my desk, the stickman surrounded by ripple like lines indicating the relationships we've explored and their proximity to him, I took a deep breath - the gap was families.

What can we learn about grown ups through our family dynamics?

This is going to be a toughy!

CHAPTER 11

It's a family affair

What does being a grown up mean to you?

'Satisfaction. I've never accomplished any great things for the world but I like to think I have, with my wife, brought a happy life to our children.

Having responsibilities that aren't visible to others but make me proud and at times, worried for how our families are moving on. It also means I can just sit back and relax (sometimes) and enjoy how things are going with our kids and grandkids. Enjoying holidays with them sometimes or just my wife and I alone and relaxed.

I don't wish I'd done more but of course there are things I could have done better.

I don't really feel 'grown up' because I don't believe, in many ways, that I have. I'm older and less moveable but slowness is comfortable, and fun comes in different ways.

Fun is the key.'
Survey Respondent

I have shared a fair bit about my parents and my partner Jim in this book, or at least I feel I have. And yet exploring the idea of grown ups in families feels quite dangerous. I am nervous to share too much or over analyse ongoing relationships. What if I were to take a view that my sister doesn't share, or describe a situation with my brothers that I have misremembered. What if I were to name a feeling that my parents weren't aware of and hurt them.

It feels there is more at risk in this chapter than in any other - even the one about work!

I have mentioned to a few people that I am struggling with this chapter, and every one of them has reacted with a sense of discomfort. Sharp intakes of breath, awkward smiles, or a burst of nervous laughter. Everyone seems to think it is a spikey question to try and answer - what is it to be a grown up in family relationships?

I wonder if this is perhaps because so much in families goes unsaid. There is generally a lot of water under the bridge. For most people these are the people who have seen everything. My family knew me as the bossy, bolshy and, I suspect, precocious young child. They will remember me as the little girl desperate for her elder sister's approval. The young teen who hid that she was bullied and instead acted at home as though everything were fine. They've seen me at my worst and at my silliest. They will have witnessed the versions of me that I would rather forget and the versions of me I'd love to meet again. They were usually within a few minutes of me from birth to nineteen when I moved away, and my grown up mask doubled in its coverage.

And I have seen all these versions of them too.

And it can be difficult to separate the person we know now from the person we knew all those years ago. Especially when, oh so often, adults revert to a version of their younger selves when in their parent's home or alongside their families. Mum always laughs because when we return home, all five of us stand and stare into the fridge - like the hungry indecisive teenagers we all were.

I so look forward to visiting my family - and yet, it's perhaps only a couple of days before I am ready to leave and head back to my own life. I wonder if this is because I devolve somewhat when I am there. I become all the younger versions of myself in response to the environment and the people. I wonder if there are versions of me that show up that I dislike, or like less than who I am now. I know I have a short fuse when I am in my parents' house - way shorter than anywhere else. I get frustrated easily and bite unnecessarily. I also feel the need to fill my folks in on everything that has happened in my life, despite speaking on the phone a few times a week, and so I talk incessantly.

And, at the same time, I am different than I used to be. And to lean again on Berne's Transactional Analysis I am probably far more adult with my parents than I am either of the child ego states. I think at times this can be unsettling for them and for my siblings. And at times it is probably a welcome relief. I have helped my parents have some important conversations, conversations they were struggling to have alone. The diplomat or mediator that I have often played amongst my siblings has now extended to my parents too.

What can be hard, as an adult visiting family, is the dual loyalties. The loyalty to the people we are now, and the loyalty to the roles in the family we are used to playing. Something in us doesn't want to shake the well worn family equilibrium by shifting our role. Maybe that's what's tricky sometimes for me, having moved away at just 19, while all the others stayed close; perhaps my loyalty to the person I am now is stronger than the desire to keep the balance. Perhaps I am more different now to the person I was when I left than I realise.

I also feel different, not just from the person I was, but from my siblings. On a recent call with my sister she also mentioned that we all have different relationships with each other, and crucially will receive exactly the same words differently from different siblings. Something that my little brother may say to her she can take with a pinch of salt where as if I said it to her, the exact same words, it would crush her, and if our older brother said it she would crush him. She said that 'we are all different - but you are the adult among us - we all go to you for advice or support.' I noticed a weird feeling when she said this, a sense of pride mixed with some embarrassment. I always want to be useful where I can but I always carry a fear that it comes with an air of superiority.

In case you are wondering, I am the middle child. I have a brother and sister above me and a brother and sister below me respectively. It's not surprising that I feel and perhaps am different. As I said, I moved away at 19 and have made a life in a different part of the country, working in an industry I never knew existed, exposing myself to experiences, people, foods, activities and much more that I may never have done had I stayed in my hometown - not because they don't exist there but because I may not have continued on the journey of risk taking and exploration if I hadn't made that first big leap. I'm also sure that, like Sharon, I have ADHD which also explains a felt sense of difference. I often feel that I see or hold situations in a more 3D or multi dimensional way to my family - this has always helped me when mediating childhood clashes. Lastly, two years of my life that I regard as some of my most formative were in a school, an environment that no one else experienced. My little brother went to the same school actually but when we reminisce we could be describing completely separate worlds. Moving to this school at fourteen allowed me to be me - not embarrassed by or bullied for my smarts but pushed to challenge them.

And all of this, and much more, adds up to a difference that is no better, or worse. It's not good or bad. It's just different. And difference can bring with it flavour, and fear.

Most of the time, when I visit, I stay with my parents and my siblings usually come to their house too to visit with me and the boys. Sometimes there can be an uncomfortable air between my sister and I when we are both at our folks house. I get the impression she feels like I am judging her or waiting to trip her up. I imagine she feels she is entering a clique of my parents and I, like we've been talking about her before her arrival and will again after she leaves. I think it can be tricky for both of us - perhaps we are both walking on eggshells in those visits. We want to enjoy our time together, but sometimes something gets in the way.

Recently I was heading home for a weekend and, through poor planning on my part, my parents were going to be away. I asked my elder sister if the boys and I could stay at her house instead. Her lads are older than mine and my little ones had been desperate for a sleepover with their cousins so it seemed like a win win. In the lead up to our visit I started to get nervous. I was worried about a whole weekend of eggshells, a whole weekend of awkward moments where our differences in food, TV, and interests would be pointed out. Later she told me that she had also been nervous too.

Our nerves were in vain. We had an incredibly easy weekend together, no eggshells once we'd settled in. No upsets, no sense of judgement on either part. We had some quality conversations about ourselves, our lives, our choices and our challenges. Neither of us became defensive. It was real. It was unexpected.

I wonder if being on her turf stopped both of us from reverting back to our younger selves, replaying decade old relational habits. It allowed us to be ourselves, who we are now - and in doing so we found a common ground of adult to adult 'like', above the rich soil of unconditional 'love'.

* * * * *

If I were to criticise my family in any way, myself included, it's that I don't think we have the tough conversations early enough, or well enough. I often feel that as a family we avoid them until they have escalated to an emotional boiling point. We hope that they will just go away, dissolve into the everyday. I see this in other families too. Adult children and their parents avoiding confrontation or disagreement beyond every day banter and mickey taking. When confrontation happens, huge rifts can form. I know of siblings who, as adults, have cut each other out of their lives, exchanging Christmas cards at best. Sometimes this division comes from just seeing the world differently and expressing that. Families were divided over Brexit, divided over Trump, divided over Covid and their beliefs about what was right or wrong in all of those cases.

My knee jerk reaction is that families dividing and ceasing to be in relationship with each other is very sad - the 'blood is thicker than water' argument. But is that view just coming from a societal pressure that families should stay together and stand by each other? We should spend Christmases together, speak often and visit when we can. Does that result in people being together when they don't want to be? Are we trying to create the Hollywood Christmas films where everyone is joyous in their togetherness and matching pyjamas?

My other reaction to families who cut ties is one of admiration. They haven't bought into the Christmas movies or forced relationships to continue when they don't serve any party. A friend of mine never sees her brother - and I mean ever. Not because there was a falling out; they just don't like each other very much. If they weren't siblings they wouldn't be friends, so they don't see any point in hanging out.

And yet I also know siblings who despised each other when they were younger and are now effectively best friends - holidaying together with their families. For some people their childhood families will always be tough and triggering and they may not be able to be themselves with parents or siblings. Accepting that, mitigating for it, protecting themselves or building in decompression time after any visit may also be utterly grown up.

But there seem to be four things at play in most families - a sense of obligation to be together, a genuine unconditional love of one another, varying degrees of liking each other and lastly, liking each other but not wanting to be around them very much. Mix that all up into a high stakes Christmas environment and it can be the recipe for a feast, or for a beast. And unlike in friendships or working relationships that have run their course, the links through blood or name or history can make any parting feel much more drastic. You can't just let a sibling relationship drift then bump into each other in the street a decade on and both laugh saying 'Gosh, it's been ages! How are you?'

I wonder if that is what is at risk in my family, and the reason we don't always have the tough conversations. We all feel loved by each other - that will never be at risk. But maybe the friendships we hope to have with our siblings and parents are at risk if we upset them. Perhaps the 'love' is unconditional but the 'like' isn't? Perhaps, as we learnt through exploring grown up friendships and grown ups at work, it is authenticity to who we really are when in our family units that is a quality of a grown up - and both the riskiest and hardest thing to maintain?

And let's not over intellectualise this. Maybe it is utterly authentic and beautiful to occasionally shed all of our adult responsibilities when we visit with our families and instead just stare into the fridge wondering what to pick at in order to spoil our dinner.

*****

In our conversation, my sister also mentioned that the challenge when we come together can be the different ways we parent our kids. What we will stand for, the language we use, the allowances we make, the hard lines we stand by. While with friends I see often I feel comfortable and confident to 'parent' their kids when I am closest, and wouldn't bat an eye at them doing the same with mine, I spend less time with my siblings - we don't have the innate understanding of what's ok and what's not - so we all stand back and just get quietly frustrated instead.

This made me think of another type of family which may come to mind in this question - the one in which I am actually the parent. Me, Jim and our two boys - our untidy little family unit of four. What does it mean to be the grown up in this scenario? Well, first of all, it means occasionally saying in a fit of frustration 'I am the grown up!' but I suspect it's more than that. It's probably more than being the person who uses the sharp knives, gets things out of the oven and drives the car too.

So who better to ask than children? When I asked groups of ten year-olds they told me that grown ups go to work, pay the bills and essentially stop them doing what they want to do. But when I asked my son and some of his friends what makes their mummies and daddies grown ups they spoke of cooking dinner, giving hugs, occasional silliness, wearing bigger shoes, and deciding what they do together. He was only four at the time. But it's an interesting mix, with the headline for me being the person with a sense of 'responsibility'.

Our parenting styles will likely be driven by the way we want our children to behave, our family units to work and the types of adults we hope they will grow into. It will be shaped by how we were parented, what we experienced as kids. And of course it will be highly influenced by the child themselves and their responses to our styles. I wondered what researchers before have deemed as the most important attributes or qualities of parents and whether that would shine a light on our question about grown up families.

Diana Baumrind, a developmental psychologist, and her colleagues first named the three main parenting styles as part of a new system for classifying parenting styles in 1966. Their approach was to look at the parent's practices, particularly the way that parents attempt to control their children. Researcher Gwen Dewar also commented on this in her work in 2024. The three styles were named as:

- **Permissive parents**
  These parents are responsive and warm but resist imposing rules or setting expectations. 'They prefer to let their kids regulate themselves.' Dewar states.

- **Authoritarian parents**
  These parents require blind obedience of their children and demonstrate less warmth and sensitivity. 'They attempt to enforce compliance through punishments, threats, and psychological control.'

- **Authoritative parents**
  These parents are responsive and warm, avoiding over the top punishments like the permissive parents but do set clear expectations. They create a sense of freedom within a framework. Clear boundaries within which the child can assert their autonomy and control. They are in conversation with the child and use reasoning to help the child develop understanding and empathy.

Later in 1983 Maccoby and Martin added a fourth style - The Uninvolved or Neglectful parents.

Dewar suggested that if a parent wants to raise independent, self-reliant and socially competent adults that an authoritative style is best. She defined an authoritative style as 'an approach to child-rearing that combines warmth, sensitivity, and the setting of limits. Parents use positive reinforcement and reasoning to guide children. They avoid resorting to threats or punishments.' This sounds great and is probably the style of parenting I aspire to, although we do use consequences and therefore the threat of consequences in our house. TV or pudding may be taken away if undesirable behaviours persist. I think we learned the hard way that we weren't setting enough limits, particularly with our eldest when it was just him. I am a very laid back person so I would happily roll with the changes on the days we spent together, only later realising I'd not really encouraged him to see things through.

I fear that I am writing this with a bias toward the parenting style that I have chosen (or that came about in our house) but I absolutely know some Permissive parents who live a wonderful, emergent and incredibly close life with their children. I can picture some authoritarian parents, particularly in old TV shows, and know that when I am not at my best I would love to have an hour or two of blind obedience. To say 'we're off to do blah blah jump in the car' and just have a child hop off the sofa and head to the car would be a gift! And I suspect this style works for some people and works for some kids. However, there isn't a clear style of parenting that denotes grown upness here. I could argue that being in conversation with a child rather than dictating to them does feel more grown up to me - but like I said, it's bitten me in the arse a few times too. I decided to persist for a moment longer on this topic and looked into what is important for children in their parents' behaviours, what supports them in their development.

An answer came to me through the research of Lippold and colleagues in 2016 which showed that, over a controlled period, 'consistency [of parenting style] was significantly correlated with three indicators of youth adjustment'. These indicators were; Youth Risk Behaviour - taking over the top and unnecessary or dangerous risks - Youth Depressive Symptoms - a proclivity toward depression and anxiety - and Youth Physical Symptoms - for example headaches, tiredness, fluctuation or extremes of appetite.

This research was carried out with a large group of children of similar demographics in the US. The headline finding was that one way to best serve our children is through consistency - not bouncing too often between parenting styles, something I suspect I do more often than I might care to admit.

What I don't think this means is that we can't be human too. We can of course make mistakes, and owning that in front of the kids has got to be a good thing too right? Showing them that mistakes are ok and that we can all recover from them? Surely that is a behaviour of a grown up? Consistency doesn't have to mean being exactly the same all the time, instead it is about children having a sense of expectation in terms of our reactions to certain situations. Back to Wayne being himself at home and at work, being congruent with his colleagues - I think this consistency comes from understanding who you are and where you stand on certain things, what your tolerance is for accidents or risk. I am, mostly, consistent in living my values with my kids. Accidents happen while rudeness is not ok. Fun can be found in any situation - but it needs to be in context of the situation. Love will be given often and freely. And there is always work to be done right? If I am trying to create a sense of freedom within a clear framework for them, and live it consistently, I may need to be clearer on the framework from time to time to keep us all steady.

* * * * *

The family that I grew up in is more blended than I have so far described. It is made up of my elder siblings, from my mum's first marriage - they then have a little sister from their father's second marriage. My younger brother and I followed via our mum and dad, and much later we welcomed our much younger sister who joined us at 13 when she was fostered by my parents.

My parents fostered for around twenty years from when I was 17. Over those years I have returned to a house full of toys, noise and joys - often with different little faces at the breakfast table. But Charlie, our little sister, stuck around until she went off to University and then moved away to start her career in East Anglia. To all of our relief she too returns to Mum and Dad's house to stare into the fridge, laze on the sofa and be generally parented once again. She's one of us.

In this chapter I could have considered many of the families we encountered through fostering over those twenty years, but in truth what often seemed to be lacking was a grown up. Children came to my parent's home because they weren't being looked after very well, or loved enough - sometimes this simply wasn't within the grasp of the biological parents through addiction, their own trauma or simply their capabilities. Often the stories were sad, but the children who appeared out of those stories were wonderful. And in our different ways we all tried to make them feel a part of the family while they were with us. Just extra nieces or nephews to my siblings and I, and playmates for our kids. Many have gone on to be adopted and some have been happily reunited with their biological parents. Quite a few have kept in touch with my parents through emails, calls and even annual visits - one little boy (who's not so little anymore) messaged my mum on mother's day, a good 15 years after he left her as a preschooler. It's beautiful and I feel immensely proud of my parents for their part in the lives of these families.

No family is conventional when you get into it, we all have our lumps and bumps, but I wondered what we might learn from a very different type of family story, one that started in a very different time, and what it might tell us about grown ups. So I spoke to Ann.

Ann's story

At age thirty-nine Ann gave birth to her miracle baby. After years of trying, Steven arrived.

When Ann was around 36 weeks pregnant the baby's growth paused and her doctors recommended they induce her, get labour started and care for the little one out in the open. On arrival a 6lb Steven was whisked off to the special care unit and popped straight into an incubator for safe keeping. It all happened in such a hurry that Ann wasn't initially aware that she could see him. She sat on her bed, worried and desperate to hold her new baby. After a while, a nurse noticed an anxious Ann hadn't moved and almost sarcastically said to her 'you can go and visit him you know!?!' She was off like a shot! On arriving on his ward she was met by a tiny baby, orange with jaundice, his eyes tight shut, not a single eyelash there to define them. He was a 'grunter' apparently, a technical term, due to the little pig-like noises he made as he was helped to breathe; but utterly beautiful. Ann fell in love on the spot.

It was a few days until he opened his eyes and it happened as she held him: 'his eyes just popped open and looked up at me,' she said as she regaled me with her story. He was in hospital for ten days, not much compared to some but an age for any new parents. At one of the early morning visits, as she looked longingly at the baby she had worked so hard for, the nurses began asking her and new Dad Reg about their families' medical histories. Not unusual questions, not tricky for most, perhaps not a conversation that other mothers would recollect even having had, but for Ann this was a life-changing moment.

Ann had reached the age of thirty-nine with only the knowledge that her father was an engineer in the US Air Force serving in England during the Second World War. 'A nice and kind man who died in a plane crash on his return journey,' her mother had told her. She had never needed to know more than this, never felt the need for a father even - until now. As she stood in the hospital cradling a tiny Steven it felt her lack of answers to these questions left her baby exposed. Ann told me that this was the moment she decided she would try and find out more about her dad.

But life goes on, and life with a small child goes quicker than you'd expect. Baby Steve learned to breathe on his own, feed and, in time, walk, talk, play football and climb trees. He was a perfectly normal, wonderful little boy. Utterly unaffected by the blank spots in Ann's knowledge. The itch however did not go away; she suspected that at some point this information would be asked for again and she wanted to be equipped.

With so many 'war babes' - illegitimate children of American or Canadian soldiers - the War Office had been inundated with requests for information and, for reasons we can only speculate on, when Ann wrote to them they became unhelpful and clammed up at her questions. A dead end. As time passed so did her immediate energy to find answers; she had a child that needed her attention, and life went on.

Ann was telling me her story over a video call on a rainy Tuesday afternoon. She was incredibly matter-of-fact, playful at times and lighthearted, full of jokes and acceptance, but not overly emotional - even about the heavy stuff. This is how I had always known her. My Aunty Ann had married my dad's brother, Reg, when the two of them were just eighteen and they, along with my cousin Steve, are present in many of my early memories. Holidaying together, BBQing at home, camping, Sunday lunches and general family fun. Ann was probably the family member most involved with us as we were kids. While the other adults caught up and talked about adult stuff, Ann was making sure we had a football or paints, had stencils and books. She's the same now with my children. An honorary Granny whose suitcase seems as full of art stuff and stickers for my boys as it is her packed with her clothes when she comes to visit. She is someone who just loves being around kids, and they love being around her.

An only child born to an unmarried Irish mother in war torn London, a deceased father and surrounded by an ugly attitude toward the Irish. You might imagine her stories to be gritty and a little bitter, filled with unfairness and discrimination - but that isn't her way. Ann takes joy in remembering the good stuff and can't see the point in hanging on to the bad.

In 1943, a twenty-one-year-old Enda fell pregnant with Ann having met Oscar James Gast in church one Sunday and courted him whenever he was in London. 'I think he was a lost love to her; it wasn't a fling - it was more than that.' Her family back in Ireland expected her, no, strongly encouraged her, to give up the baby, to which Enda replied firmly and clearly that she would not. 'My mum wouldn't be told what to do so people didn't try telling her twice.' Enda accepted that life was likely to be hard but better hard and together than hard and apart.

Shortly after Ann's birth, and the details aren't clear how, Enda was offered a job as a maid in a manor house in Windsor called Orchard Lea. The lady of the house, known only as Lady Bath, took in three unmarried mothers and their babies in 1944 and saved them from the awful mother and baby homes that dotted the countryside. Homes where mothers were shamed and threatened, babies often adopted out from under them. So much has come to light about these homes over the last twenty or so years, stories of abuse and exploitation, and though Enda may not have known it at the time – she had had a lucky escape. Lady Bath gave the girls a home, a job with a small income and allowed them to have their babies with them as they moved around the house cleaning and tidying.

'Lady Barff, as I apparently called her, saved us,' Ann told me, speaking with such adoration of a woman she doesn't remember but owes so much to.

At two years old Ann and her mum were invited to move back to London. Her mum's newly married sister had offered to look after little Ann during the day so that Enda could work, giving the little family an opportunity for stability and to create a home of their own. They jumped at the chance. For years Enda would drop Ann off at her sister's in the morning and pick her up in the evening, stopping only for tea and a catch up on a Friday when she didn't have work the following day. Staying for tea meant more play time for Ann with her younger cousin Linda and a chance to see her uncle. Ann's uncle was the only man she really knew outside of the teachers at school. He was a calm and quiet man, but always kind and, despite some traditional values, he was always without judgement of her mum's illegitimate situation. 'He was a fair man,' Ann told me. 'If there was only one sweet left he would give me a knife to cut it in half and Linda and I would share – he taught us to always share and to stand by each other.'

The absence of a father wasn't obvious to Ann particularly, and she was well into primary school before she came home confused one day and asked her mum what dads were for.

'They go out to work and earn the money,' Enda had replied in her thick, bouncy Irish accent.

'But you do that?' said a confused Ann.

'They do the decorating and fix things around the house,' pushed Enda.

'But you do that too Mum?' questioned Ann.

'Then I suppose I don't know - we probably don't need one,' stated Enda. Ann accepted this and, according to her, she never wondered about dads again. 'Me and mum got on fine. She worked, I went to school, we had the odd treats, and we were close to my aunt, uncle and cousin. And my Granny was in London too, so we had a family. I never felt I was missing anything. I did feel different though, different to the other kids because they had dads. But as I didn't know what they were for, I was different but not lacking.'

Ann said that her mum never once said a bad word about her father, in fact he wasn't a big topic of conversation for them. Even into her teens if the subject would arise her mum would either close it down or talk without detail about how wonderful he was and how much he loved them both. She told Ann that he had met her when she was little and was such a proud father that he had taken her out in the pram - not a common sight in 1944. If Ann had thought about timelines or challenged these recollections, she may have noticed the discrepancies, but there was no need. The stories were nice, they felt nice, and they didn't hurt anyone. Hers was an upbringing not without its challenges but full of love and fun - who could want for more, who needed a dad?

Enda even waited until Ann was married herself before she courted again: 'she said she never wanted a man to come between us, so she waited, then just as I was due to marry Reg she married Les, who just happened to be the father of a friend of mine from school. Les was wonderful, we had known him for years and mum supported him when his first wife became ill and passed. They were great friends, and it felt very natural when mum and Les married, I loved him dearly.'

Back to the search. In 1995, after the War Office had gone silent, Ann came across an article in the local paper about a woman named Shirley McGlade. Shirley had discovered a way of finding the American fathers of War Babes and, through her connections with the Veterans Office, had found eleven fathers so far. Ann got in touch and told her all she knew about her dad. A short time later a letter arrived. Oscar James Gast had died, but not on his return to the states. He died at his home in Alabama in 1966 some twenty years later. Ann put the letter away in a drawer, along with any thoughts or questions, and carried on with life.

Ann had always wanted to have a big family, to have children all around her, but when that didn't happen for her she embraced her role as Steve's mum and served her need by becoming a teacher. For thirty years Ann taught in a special needs school in Southwest London, working with some incredibly fun kids, if a little challenging at times.

A year later, when randomly sorting through some papers she came across the letter again. This time she looked more closely at a note right at the bottom. Oscar's next of kin - Oscar James Gast. 'I couldn't believe it, I had a brother!' she told me. 'It had never crossed my mind that I might have siblings and now I potentially had a brother.'

After some time and consideration, she optimistically wrote to the address on the letter, mindful that it had been the address of her brother in 1966, nearly thirty years before, and he had almost certainly moved on. A couple of months passed, and nothing came back, she accepted that her trail had run dry and, as is her way, carried on with life.

Opening the front door to an empty house after work on the 12th February 1996 'I can remember the date Sam,' she told me, she was stopped by a large yellow 'air mail' envelope sitting on top of the other post, and on the corner a return name and address 'Gast.' 'Oh shit, I thought, oh shit, this is from them, whoever they are.'

The first page of a wad of papers was a letter from a woman named Dorothy. It started 'Dear Ann, firstly your father is not dead.'

Although the details had changed over the years she had never once considered that her father might not actually be dead, and that first revelation was enough to floor her. 'But he is very unwell,' continued Dorothy. The Oscar James who died in 1966 had been Ann's grandfather who shared her father's name, and her father was the named next of kin she had assumed was a brother.

The letter explained how Oscar James, known as OJ, returned to Alabama after the war to his wife and told her about Baby Ann in London. His wife had demanded he choose between them, it would be her or the baby. Having recently miscarried and being in a state of deep depression OJ felt he should stand by her and support her. Sadly, after having a daughter together two years later, the relationship deteriorated and they divorced leaving him with sole custody of Ann's younger sister Martha. 'Oh, shit I have a sister!' Ann said to me.

When her sister was 15, OJ got remarried to Dorothy who herself had two children. 'He was a wonderful father to all of them and went on to adopt her children Donna and Marilyn, Dorothy told Ann.

'I have three sisters!' The two of them then went on to have another two children together - David and Missy.

In one letter Ann had gained a father, a stepmother, three half siblings and two adopted siblings. Now one of six, she was a far cry from the only child she had grown up being. And of course, these siblings had children, on her father's side she was now aunt to many nieces and nephews, one of whom was also called Steven.

On receiving Ann's letter, Dorothy had called the children together and told them all about her. She herself had always known about Ann, her father had spoken of the baby he had left in London and how he loved her. So, Enda had been right about that - she was loved by her father despite him never having met her. At the family meeting they all agreed that they wanted to meet Ann, that they wanted to have her as a sister. They clubbed together and wanted to pay for her, Reg and Steve to fly over to Alabama as soon as possible and meet their father before he passed. By this point, blind and unable to speak, OJ was close to the end.

The year before Ann had lost her stepdad Les to an aggressive cancer. It had been painful to watch and she was reluctant to have the only memory of her real father be one in which he was full of pain and close to death too. Instead, she phoned. She explained to Dorothy that she was unable to come that quickly due to work commitments and they instead planned a trip for the May. Dorothy held the phone to her father's ear. Ann has no memory at all of what she actually said to him 'it is all a bit of a blur,' she told me 'but he made some noises in response.' And when the phone returned to Dorothy, she told Ann that he had smiled and had tears running down his cheeks.

OJ died before Ann and her family landed in Alabama two months later.

Ann visited her mother on the South coast of England the weekend of the phone call to tell her about the letter and about the family. She was nervous, she had no idea how her mum would react after so long. After lots of small talk and avoidance Enda eye-balled her and said 'So why are you really here then?'

'My mum didn't mince her words,' Ann told me. 'I told her everything and she sat and listened, taking it all in quietly. When I finished, I asked her how she felt and braced myself. For what, I didn't know. Mum said that she was so glad I would have someone after she was gone.'

As my aunt told me this part of her story, I felt my eyes welling up remembering Enda. I had met her when I was little quite a few times and although I didn't know her well, I had always liked this slightly crazy Irish woman my cousin called Granny, she always seemed to be laughing.

Now I saw a generosity in her that was quite beautiful. Enda, having never said a bad word about the man, having lost him as much as Ann if not more when he returned to the states, had no bitterness or self-pity. She didn't look to keep her daughter to herself, or to suggest anything other than joy at the prospect of Ann having more people in her life to love and be loved by. Enda had worked hard her whole life to give Ann a home that didn't need a father in it, to give her a family that lacked nothing, to give her an environment where she could grow strong and be proud of who she was. And now she was also willing to share her daughter, her reason for being, with strangers on a farm halfway across the world.

Ann, Reg and a thirteen-year-old Steve, touched down in Alabama and drove to Marilyn's house. 'Everyone was there to meet us. It was a huge family! I met Dorothy, my father's second wife and she couldn't have been more pleased to see me, like my mum there was no jealousy, bitterness or negativity - she was just so happy for us all. We hugged. Then I met my sister Martha who Dad had had with his first wife after returning from London. I learned that he had insisted her middle name be Ann as a way of keeping me close. Martha had always known about me and known that her middle name was mine. She wasn't cold toward me but perhaps a little wary.' Martha died in 2023 but thankfully she and Ann had got to know each other and developed a sisterly relationship despite their rocky start.

'Then there was Donna and Marilyn who welcomed me with open arms, then my brother David and then finally I locked eyes with my youngest sister Missy. Missy walked straight over to me and said 'I always wondered who I looked like, now I know.' I'd never looked like anyone before, it wasn't something I was prepared for. Siblings often resemble each other but I hadn't thought about it in advance. Now I was looking at a woman I had never met and seeing flashes of myself in her face.'

'Steven too now had buckets of cousins who all immediately took him into the fold. I had a moment when I was inside chatting with my new family and Steve was outside with all the cousins playing basketball. I remember it felt weird, wonderful, but weird.'

After their first emotional visit the five Alabama siblings, who had each inherited 6 acres of their father's farm, agreed to give Ann one acre each, meaning they all had an even five acres. For the umpteenth time in this story, I was struck by the unpredictability of it. My expectation was that at some point there would be a bad guy. Someone would get upset, someone would get protective, someone would shun her or close down on her. But there was none. In a tale that spanned over 50 years by this point, included an illegitimate baby in a time of war to an Irish Catholic migrant, a Lady of the upper class, marriage, lies, illness, death, parenthood and land ownership - and I'm sure much more - there was no villain. Just example after example of people taking each other as they are, giving each other the benefit of the doubt, loving without condition.

I had tried to stay quiet while she had told me her story, which jumped backwards and forward in time and bounced from deeply revealing to playful and jovial. At times I pushed her for more. Ann has a habit of stating the facts and I often wondered if there was more behind what she was saying than she let on. When she was finished, we both took a deep breath. 'That was more emotional than I thought it would be Sam,' she said to me, inhaling again and letting out her loud signature laugh.

Ann now holds dual nationality and visits her siblings often. It keeps her busy though, being one of six!

In this story, I struggle to see anyone not behaving like a grown up: Enda's selfless generosity of her only daughter discovering a long lost family. A step mother demonstrating nothing but love for a long lost child. Siblings excited to have one more person to split their attention and inheritance with. And Ann, forgiving of the actions of a young man at war and walking into a new life with openness and vulnerability.

Perhaps what we can learn about grown ups in this story, is that they know the world is bigger than them, and that life is longer than circumstance - they don't waste time or energy on grudges or competition, instead give it generously to the opportunity for connection and the potential for love. They are filled with compassion for the beautiful, messy, fallible, incredible and imperfect humans around them. Perhaps the grown ups in this family chose to care for each other rather than care for anything else.

CHAPTER 12

One last Grown up

Jay's story

While on holiday with my family in 2023 I received a text from someone who I'm not sure had ever texted me before. In fact I had only met Dave about three times.

The first I barely recall as we were all drunk and celebratory. He was the new boyfriend of Jay, a friend of mine, visiting Bath to see her and meet some of her friends!

The second was at their wedding in Padstow, an incredible celebration of love and fun, set in the grounds of a beautiful castle.

The third was when the pair returned to Bath with their beautiful baby Dora. A tough birth and a tricky start aside, she was gorgeous, and they, the perfect new family.

Every time I met Dave it had been at a significant moment in his relationship with Jay, and looking back now I feel honoured to have been a part of those moments. He always struck me as a genuinely nice person, not overly chatty but warm hearted, playful. A man making the most of a happy life, helped in no small part by his bouncy, colourful and extroverted wife who makes life look like something delicious to take big bites out of!

Despite not having a lot of them in my life, I love them both dearly.

His text invited me to a surprise 40th birthday party for Jay. Despite it being only a couple of weeks away, meaning a night in a hotel, and leaving my partner home with the kids, I knew I was going to do all I could to attend as soon as I read his message. Yes, for Jay, of course! I wanted to be there for her, to party with her and to celebrate with her. But just as much for Dave. I knew what it would mean to him if he managed to collar a friend from Bath for the party, it would be a win. And I think he needed one.

Jay had grown up in Padstow, a real Cornish girl, obsessed with the May Day celebrations, the sea and the rolling hills all around. A seven-year-old Jay met fellow Padstonian, Tracey and they quickly became friends. Tracey's parents were desperate for her to enjoy the ponies they kept, but she had no interest at all - Jay on the other hand was all over it. And soon she was taking any and every opportunity to hang out with her best friend, the ponies and, on occasion, Tracey's big brother Dave.

As is the case in many small towns, everyone knows everyone, and in the teenage years, everyone snogs everyone. It was certainly true in my small seaside town on the other side of the country. Jay and Dave however never had that teenage snog. Despite her crush on him and his secret crush on her, it was Dave's best friend who asked her out and became her first love. But first loves fizzle, time went by and soon Jay was away to university, popping back only occasionally to visit friends and family.

On one such journey back, it was Dave who more obviously held the torch and Jay who was trying to drunkenly set him up with a work friend visiting with her for the weekend.

Back and forth the attraction went, inconveniently cropping up when one or other had partners and neither was aware of the other yoyo-ing in and out of crushes. And at some point in this yoyo-ing Dave got married.

Until May Day in 2010 when finally, their stars aligned. May Day in this small harbour town is a big deal. The streets erupt in flowers and greenery, music, dancing and singing. Everyone, of all ages, wears gleaming white outfits with blue or red trim to greet the summer together. The Obby Oss Festival, as it's also known, is a celebration of the Celtic feast of Beltane and honours the approaching season. It's a time for joy and gratitude for the good weather ahead. And for most people an opportunity to come together with neighbours and friends to dance and sing, to drink and be merry!

For Jay and Dave that year - little did they know there too was a summer ahead for them.

Toward the end of a day of festivities, when the town was gathered for the final ritual, the drums boomed and chatter and laughter filled the air. Dave's then soon-to-be ex-wife stood across from the childhood friends and began snogging her new bloke in front of the gossiping horde. Small towns love salacious stories like that more than anything, and Jay, spotting Dave's pain, couldn't stand for him to be humiliated. Like any good friend would, she grabbed him by the scruff of his blue neckerchief and, planting her own kiss, started local tongues wagging in a very new direction.

As in any good romcom, the kiss began as a theatrical show for the crowd, over the top and performative, but quickly became a moment in which, I imagine, the crowd dissolved and the two of them were alone for a moment - meeting each other as if for the first time. In my imagination the music softened around them and the cider drinkers fell silent, reverent in the presence of love. But I also know Padstow on May Day and it's more likely that they were bumped and jostled until their lips parted.

Finally, they'd cracked it!

Both single, both besotted with each other and both in the same place at the same time - well sort of.

Jay was living four hours away and working a further three when they kicked off their long overdue relationship and Dave was part way through a divorce. But these are minor details when falling in love. By the following February Jay had moved into his cottage on the hill, and their life together started, with a view of the bay.

When I went hunting for stories of grown upness Jay messaged me instantly. I was pleased but a little nervous. I wasn't sure if it was the right time for her, I wasn't sure if I was a good enough interviewer to navigate her story respectfully enough. We set up a time to speak and I tried to prepare myself as best I could.

I needn't have bothered.

'So I've been reflecting a lot on this,' she started without missing a beat, 'and actually, you writing this book and putting the question of 'grown ups' out there, coincided with, or maybe was the catalyst for, me starting to be really curious about what I considered my own definition of being a grown up.' I was in shock. With women like Jay I often notice my imposter syndrome bubble up. Through none of her doing, I can begin to feel inadequate, I question my value in the conversation, or even in the friendship. Like many of my childhood friendships, I simply don't feel 'cool' enough.

When I first met Jay she seemed to me to be someone who had their shit together. She was a funny and confident woman with a great job, a nice flat and an eclectic group of friends. I remember feeling a little intimidated by her even then actually. At the time I was trying to work out who I was, and floundering. I was in a weird relationship, working in an unfulfilling environment and not quite feeling like I was making the most of myself and my life. But she was smashing it, she was a grown up, or so I had thought.

And here she was, sitting in her home office, the sun streaming in and seagulls squawking in the background, telling me that without even realising it I had had a profound impact on her.

It was around the time that I had put this question out into the world that Jay was going through a promotion process at work, a process that included the people around her giving their opinions of her. People she managed, people who led her, clients and partners - and there was a theme. From every direction she heard a loud and consistent message 'When there is a crisis, you need Jay'.

'That feedback told me that something had changed in who I am, and how I turn up, that I wasn't consciously aware of. A change that has enabled me and equipped me to deal with all of the awful things that have happened, and if I was to put a label on it - I'm now a grown up.'

I wanted to know what life before this change looked and felt like to her, but I barely had to ask - she read my mind and took me back to her childhood and adolescence. 'For years, I have been resisting being a grown up,' she began. 'In fact, I have resisted giving into aspects of my personality because they felt too grown up. My mum, for instance, was a very tidy person and always needed the house to be straight. As a teenager I noticed the same need in me, I knew that I operated better when the house or flat was clean and clear - but I resisted it.' Jay was laughing at herself as she spoke, beaming down the camera at me. 'Having a tidy house was too much like a grown up, too much like my mum.'

She was drawn to responsibility as a lens on the subject. She described her realm of responsibility then as being fairly close, 'just the things that needed to get done really', the day to day and the surface level. She ticked off the things that needed doing but not through choice, through necessity. And as Jay has always had the ability to problem-solve, stay calm and be pragmatic she often found herself in situations that called for 'a grown up', she would look around and notice that no one else was stepping up 'so it had to be me'. I recognised myself in her story and we shared examples back and forth of times when the proverbial was hitting various fans and everyone else stood waiting, so you take one for the team. But after a while it can feel like you're taking an awful lot for the team and too often.

We talked about how, at times, she resented it; resented not being able to be a passenger or a child while someone else took the reins. As I listened to her and tried my hardest to stay in her story, I was distracted by my own experiences. We'd had a busy few years, Jim and I, and although I willingly took charge, when I was emotionally drained and dog tired, I often wanted someone else to swoop in and save the day. In truth though, I'm not sure I always left (or maybe leave) a lot of room or opportunity for people to do this - and I likely don't seem like I want or need help. The conversation went quiet, and we both paused for a moment to think about that, about how much we accidentally encourage others to be dependent on us. Perhaps we don't have faith in them, or perhaps it's a role we've created for ourselves.

But there was one example where Jay hadn't encouraged it, hadn't wanted it at all.

In 2017 Jay's mum passed away after an awful accident. It was unexpected and heartbreaking for their family. Jay hadn't long become a mum herself and was now cannoned into the matriarch role within the family. When describing what had happened Jay felt she should have been allowed to be a child at that time - she was thirty-three but that had nothing to do with it, she was her mum's child, her mum's baby. She should have been allowed to grieve, to wallow - to just be a child losing a parent. Instead, her dad, so torn up in his own grief, ran away from the situation. 'My dad just immediately seemed to forget that it was my mum that died, and I became his best friend.' He would rely on her, like a crutch for comfort, support, light relief and at times even the fundamentals like dinners and legal formalities. 'I wanted to be looked after, but I was doing all the looking after. I wasn't given the opportunity to just be a child. In my head I was, but outwardly I had to grow up, kind of against my will.'

Poor Jay had to cope with a toddler, a busy life, and the inquest into her mum's death all while suspending her own grief - holding it in some sort of vacuum where it couldn't hurt anyone or unsettle what needed to be done.

It took a long time for Jay to put some boundaries back into her relationship with her dad but even as we chatted she was full of empathy and love for him. 'In hindsight, I wouldn't have had that any other way because he couldn't handle it, and I could - at least in the moment I could.' Jay described how later, when the dust had settled a little it all caught up with her and she suffered high levels of anxiety and panic attacks.

You might think that an ordeal like this would have prepared Jay for anything that life had to throw at her - but it didn't. It simply wasn't a long enough gap for her to digest what she'd been through and learn from it before the next swipe came.

In 2018, a year after losing her mum and with a three-year-old daughter, her incredible husband, biggest supporter and stay-at-home dad, Dave, was told he had cancer. He was just thirty-five years-old.

Jay and Dave were forced to deal with a situation neither of them could have ever imagined. Jay pulled on her grown up mask and once again did what needed to be done. She ticked all of the boxes. She made all of the calls. She appeared brave and together, while inside she felt child-like, desperate for someone else to take over and run things.

'There were at least three times when we thought we were losing him over the years.' At times it was like nothing was wrong, they were just a family living their lives together. Jay was progressing through the ranks at a global tech company, they entirely renovated their house, their daughter was growing into an incredible young lady and they had a supportive and fun group of friends around them - life, at times, was great. Until it wasn't.

Dave had multiple tumours removed, went through three rounds of chemo and immunotherapy, was hit hard with meningitis, followed by Covid and then brain surgery, and still, life went on.

Jay, however, was living on the edge. Her mental health was in tatters from needing to keep it together, from the pressure to enjoy things when they were good and react quickly and calmly to things when they went South. She was trying to live the life she would have if this disease hadn't descended on them, building an amazing career and a healthy and fun-loving mother daughter relationship, while knowing her beloved Dave would not grow old with her. Her anxiety was through the roof and she was verging on panic attacks daily. 'I now know that it's normal to experience anticipatory grief, which is grieving the life that you are now losing - I was a vegetable for months in between reluctantly coping.'

'I knew something had to change, I had to stop resisting and resenting being the grown up and grab it with both hands.' If she didn't it appeared something may crack, and it would likely be her. 'I had to take back control of all that was controllable, and let go of the things that weren't.' Jay sat down and evaluated all that was going on and what of it she could control or influence. She stopped being led by the medical professionals and instead became part of their team. 'I was with Dave 24/7, no one knew his body, his medication, his needs better than me - they even wrote on his notes 'listen to her, she knows what she's talking about'.'

She stopped being spun and controlled by the image of what being a 'good mum' looked like, doing the homework and after school clubs, and instead contracted wrap-around care with her best friend and sister-in-law, Tracey. She even stopped looking after the emotions of others when they didn't know how to speak to her or ask how she was by telling them upfront what was and wasn't up for discussion. Like Sharon, she shared the responsibilities of her relationships, her connections with others and allowed them to look after her in the way that she needed.

'I know that I am at my best when I have taken my dog for a walk on the beach, so whatever my day looks like, it will always include that.' Jay started to care about and make space for her own needs too. 'Yes, it's a lovely walk with the dog, but I needed the space to breathe and not be needed for a bit. Just for a bit.'

'The shift in my mental health was almost immediate.'

Jay described her sense of responsibility shifting. It moved from being reluctantly accountable, responsible for the things she was forced to take on, to having a calming and even exciting sense of control. And not only did her perspective around it change, but the boundaries shifted too. She moved from being responsible for her immediate surroundings - just what presented itself to her - to looking further out, widening her reach and her sense of control. At the same time, the change in coverage came inward too and she started taking responsibility for who she was and what she needed. Jay's responsibilities went from a flat list of 'to dos' to a detailed, textured sense of the world in and around her - and how she wanted to interact with it.

As she described this to me I felt her growing in her chair, shoulders rising, head shifting backwards and her whole demeanour relaxing with it. Often when we tell stories we relive the physical sense of them, and I could see it happening. She was stronger.

When Dave texted to invite me to Jay's 40th birthday party he was five years into his fight with cancer, and, after winning many battles, it seemed he was beginning to lose the war.

The party was a fantastic success - and a huge win for Dave and the family! The room behind a social club, overlooking the harbour, was rammed full of friends and family. Purple balloons adorned the doors and stage (Jay's signature colour), music was playing, and drinks were flowing. I knew no one and yet was welcomed so warmly that by the time Jay and Dave arrived I felt firmly a part of the party. Having taken her out for cocktails, Dave convinced a hungry and slightly confused Jay to pop into the social club en route to a friend's house. Hilariously, she was starting to get miffed at the lack of planning for their night out and was stumped even further as he whizzed past the public bar on his mobility scooter and around to the function room. It was only when she opened the door that she clocked what was going on.

'SURPRISE!'

Despite losing the use of his right arm, much of his coordination, at times his memory and only that week the sight in his left eye, he'd pulled it off. Without her knowing, the woman who knew everything, he had planned an amazing party for her to be at the centre of, for her to be a passenger in without any responsibility other than to have fun! Surrounded by loved ones, BBQ food, Prosecco and the town's most in demand musician!

When the two of them and their daughter took to the dance floor, holding on to each other tightly for stability in all sorts of ways, I remember feeling so glad I had come, if only to witness their love once again, first hand. It was beautiful.

Two months later, after a spell in hospital, the two were told that the brain cancer had returned and that this time there was nothing anybody could do. His prognosis was three to six months.

'I asked him what he wanted to do and he said 'drink a bottle of wine and watch Netflix' - so that's what we did. For about three days we checked in with each other to see if we were ready to talk about it - and we weren't. And then I think he started by saying 'I've got some ideas for my funeral'. And that's how we transitioned into talking about it.'

Now there was something else that she needed to take control of, life after Dave. She had seen people lose loved ones and fall into a massive void wondering what they were without that person, having nothing to look forward to - her dad's experience when losing her mum an example close to home. 'There was this moment when I recognised I needed something afterwards. There had to *be* something afterwards. So together, we made a very conscious decision to operate in two realities through the final phases of Dave's life.'

'One was to help him be optimistic and positive, and we would talk about a future that we knew wasn't going to exist, but that helped him and worked for him.' This was a playful reality in which they pretended nothing was happening, they talked about the holidays they would take and the future they would have together.

It was light-hearted and warming - and occasionally that's all they needed - the dream.

The second was one in which Dave would soon leave Jay and their daughter and they would have to go on without him. 'I planned for the reality I knew was coming.' A reality in which they needed to make the most of their time together while being conscious of what was physically and emotionally possible for them all. A reality where Dave wanted to input and influence a future that he would not be present for.

'We talked about it in bite-sized conversations over a series of weeks, discussing different contexts and circumstances. We started by talking about funeral things and then it was bigger, and bigger topics. But Dora's future was really upsetting for him, him not being in it.'

'There were things like who's going to teach her to drive? And, he'd say, 'don't get your knickers in a twist if she doesn't want to go to university. If she wants to do something different'. Some of it was kind of philosophical. Some of it was very evidence based. It was really comforting for me because I knew he'd still be with me, I'd be living a set of requests that he made.'

Part of this readying for the unstoppable was a clear action plan for the immediate days and weeks after he passed. She, Dora, Dave and all of the family knew that the moment Dave passed she would open a bottle of Champagne that Dave had bought for her, that was chilling in their fridge. They wanted to celebrate that his turmoil was over, she wanted to celebrate his life.

On the 28th of May 2024 Dave died peacefully at home, with his wife and his family around him. Jay popped the cork and through tears of grief and relief toasted him - just as he knew she would.

'We had made this plan together so that when Dave passed, time didn't stop.'

They were so well planned that rather than the need to plan the funeral and make arrangements a flow of activity simply kicked in and happened, the music had been chosen by them together, the bearers knew who they would be, the charity donations, the flowers, the wake - it was all sorted. It struck me that together Dave and Jay had created a plan that would allow her the space to grieve, the space to breathe and be a passenger to the plan.

Jay and Dora quickly initiated the next step in the plan - to jump in their newly purchased motorhome and head off to a campsite for the weekend. 'We got to the campsite, and I started chatting to people and they're like, 'oh what brings you here?' And it just came blurting out, 'well, my husband died, so we're here.'' Jay roared with laughter as she described other people's surprise with how they were handling things and what they were doing. 'People were freaking out and looking at me like I was crazy, but it was the plan.' It was the choice they'd made together.

Various other plans were in place, all of which Dave knew about. He knew of the holiday in Greece, the music festival they headed off to in August, and had supported Jay through a gruelling promotion process in 2023 so he would have pictured her returning to work in her new role. He knew that his sister was now looking after his daughter after school and that his daughter would grow up alongside cousins, cousins so close they could be siblings. Dave knew that he was loved, and that he will continue to be loved - but that their lives would go on.

When Jay got in contact to talk about her experiences with me and her relationship with being a grown up it had been around two months since Dave passed.

As we talked, we laughed and cried as she re-lived parts of her life, and it struck me that the shifts she had described were perhaps the move from 'adulting' to being an actual 'grown up'.

I posed the idea to her.

'YES!' She shouted. 'That's it! When I was adulting, stuff got done because it needed to be done, but when I consciously started taking control of my life the right stuff got done because I wanted it to.'

'It's a bit like life insurance,' she continued. 'When you get a mortgage you get life insurance because you have to - the lender makes you. But now I am insured up to the hilt because I want to know that my family and I are safe. I've gone from nonchalantly ticking the box, to doing something that helps me sleep at night.'

The irony being that often the outcome is the same.

'I credit who I am today with all of the experiences I've gone through, good and bad.' Jay summarised before heading off to a pub garden gig with her family.

'If I hadn't resisted growing up when my mum died and in the first few years of Dave's illness, I wouldn't have had the anxiety and the panic attacks, I therefore wouldn't have been provoked to try and understand myself and what Dora, Dave and I really needed. I've had experiences where I wished it wasn't happening to me. Well, that doesn't help anything. That doesn't change anything. You can either wallow in the misfortune of the moment or choose to take what you can from it and live for what you have.'

'And there's nothing as crystallising as getting told you've got six months with the person you love to get your shit together in that regard.'

INTERLUDE

Before we get into all of that...

So far in this book I have tried to share my journey of exploration; my personal inquiries, the conversations I have had with others, the research I have completed myself and the research and theories of others. The process of holding this question has challenged me constantly. It challenged the way I see and understand myself and others, challenged the way I behave and the choices I have made.

If you are reading this feeling like you have no choices, feeling like your bed is made and you must lay in it, then indulge me a little more. I want to elaborate on a story I touched on earlier in this book that could have ended very differently had I not noticed a choice.

In our chapter on love I spoke of needing to find myself and prioritise myself in order for my relationship with Jim to thrive. This is the zoomed-in story of that shift.

Due to some lifestyle choices that we have made, Jim and I have at times been financially entwined. Of course our finances are mixed up - we have a house and kids and all of that. But for a period of time I was the sole earner in the household while he focused on the kids. This isn't an uncommon situation, although historically it would have been the other way around. But this period of entanglement and reliance coincided with a downward shift in our relationship and a change in his industry that made it difficult for him to return to work should he have wanted to.

In truth, we were struggling.

Jim felt trapped by his lack of financial independence and, as depression began setting in, he felt he had no control over his life. No choices. His only option was to continue in our lives as they currently were. In feeling like he had no choice to leave he also started to wonder if he was choosing to stay, or if he was just stuck. If he still loved me and our lives or if he was incarcerated - a sort of Stockholm syndrome. I found this incredibly hard. When I looked for reassurance of his love I was often told 'I don't know'. It hurt him too. He couldn't trust his feelings and could see how he was hurting me - but it was true. He didn't know.

One day, when the sense that he had no choice got too much for me I made a choice of my own. I chose a trial separation. I knew that I would rather be alone and have a sense of clarity than stay together not knowing if love was present or would return. We'd been in love limbo for too long.

After plenty of tears, we agreed it was the right course of action and we began planning.

There were obstacles in the way and so we had to wait a few months until we could start to live more separately (still within the same house due to finances). During those few months the pressure was off. I didn't walk on eggshells because the worst that could happen was in progress - we were breaking up. I prioritised myself and the kids over his needs, leaving him to have to sort those out himself, to meet his own needs - and he did the same. I would arrange a day out and confidently ask him if he wanted to join rather than meekly hope that he would. We both began to socialise more and exercise more - feeling that we could ask for time of each other without the expectation to spend time together. My stepping back from his life made him step into it. And, as I charted an escape route for him, albeit a little tricky, his sense of being trapped seemed to dissipate too. We started to hang out together more. We had fun together again as friends. We did quizzes, watched films, had dinner - all without the sense of obligation that previously shadowed our time together. We spoke often of our separation. I was quite excited actually - not about losing him as such, but about the freedom to be selfish at times. Plus I love change and this would have been a massive one!

As the date we had agreed upon drew closer I noticed us becoming closer too. I didn't trust it at first though. I worried that it was just a stage of grief for our relationship, or a fear of the sacrifices we would both have to make in the coming months. I doubled down on the separation. If we were going to undo our decision to part then I had to know with 100% confidence that we were making a conscious choice and that we were not just dodging something difficult.

Eventually we had the conversation and we held the question - what are we choosing?

We chose to stay together. Obviously!

But we had to know we had the choice in order to make the choice. We had to know that we could break up to decide that we didn't want to. We had to agree to a life apart to realise we wanted a life together. And we continue to ask this question. In fact this is my new 'do you love me?' which used to get asked often when I felt low and uncertain. Now, when things get tough I ask 'are we still choosing this?'

It's a much better question. A grown up question.

This is probably the most grown up thing I have ever done. And for now at least, we are happily, consciously and regularly choosing this.

Up until now you, lovely reader, have been in my thoughts. I have been picturing faces I know and some I don't. I have seen you in my imagination at the till in an airport buying my book. I have seen you laughing at the title as you unwrap it on Christmas morning - giving your mum or partner an eye roll. I have replaced the book you were reading on the Tube with this as I travel, hoping one day to see someone absorbed in it on their way to work. I have imagined it on bedside tables, on desks and in backpacks. I have pictured it dog-eared, folded and scribbled in. Oh how I hope somewhere it is well worn! I have pictured you as I have shared some of my more personal stories, and as I have retold the stories of others - hoping that they are valuable to you.

I have pictured you often as I have typed and have hoped to lay my journey out for you to pick at, but now, now I invite you in.

I am speaking to you from the trains, planes, cafes and kitchen tables at which I have written, hoping that somehow, someday I will hear some answers to all of the questions I am holding for you. I wonder what you have thought and felt as you have read along with me. I am intrigued as to which moments have resonated with you, made you feel seen and understood. And which have left you confused or uncomfortable. I wonder when you have disagreed with me, or seen something I haven't. What have you seen?

I hope you have had moments away from this book where something in it has come back to you, prompting you to question, consider or challenge yourself. I hope that you have had moments where you wanted to go deeper into a subject, hear more voices and perspectives than I have shared - and if you have wanted that, that you have gone looking for them. Most chapters in this book could be entire books themselves, so follow your intrigue. Question, challenge and discuss with others.

Maybe at this point you yourself have a new definition, a sense of what it is to be a grown up and my answer is less important to you now. How I would love to hear your thoughts!

As I write this I notice a weird and unexpected comfort that all of the above, and more, will likely be true.

I began this exploration because I wanted to know the answer, but I began this book because I hoped that whatever the findings, it would be useful to others. I assumed it would be the answer that would be of most importance; but now, as I sit here thinking of you, I expect that the journey you have taken here is likely to have been even more useful than the chapters that follow this one. Like any 'coming of age' ritual, writing this book has been an ordeal for me - an exciting and amazing time but not without its tricky and testing bits. And I hope that it has prompted you to lean into something scary or uncomfortable too - as well as swim around in your own thoughts and memories.

But we haven't come all this way together for me to leave you hanging. This is not a nasty trick in which the following pages are empty ready for you to write your own reflections - that's what the margins are for. No, I think that I have, we have, landed on something...

PART 3

What is a grown up then?

CHAPTER 13

A new definition

We established fairly early on in this book that there is a difference between grown ups and adults.

To be adult is measurable in a multitude of ways; through different lenses, different cultures and different scenarios - like our jumbo jet it's complicated, but it's knowable.

To be a grown up is a far more complex and unnameable thing. It's an opinion we have of how we feel, or how we are made to feel by others. It's a sense of grown upness that emerges from a mayonnaise-like emulsification of the mindsets we hold, the things we choose to believe or challenge, the way we behave, how we interact with ourselves and the world. And like mayonnaise, we can't go into it and pull out the eggs, changing just one ingredient and expecting that *boom* we're all grown up - we're done.

What we need instead is an authentic practice of grown upness.

I love the idea of practice, it immediately says unfinished in a really positive way. Painting is a practice, DJ'ing is a practice, playing the cello is a practice, parenting is a practice - we have to work on these everyday. We practice medicine because the context of patients and medical knowledge is always changing, we practice law because the application of law shifts in response to an ever changing society, we practice being grown up because there is no end game, there is no formula, no perfect mayonnaise, only today's particular flavour.

So while I encourage us to hold the qualities of our ingredients lightly, I do feel like we can name them.

First of all, people can't be grown ups in isolation. Connection is our first grown up practice, and I invite you to consider all of the following practices with connection in mind - to self, to others and to the world. Connection doesn't mean grown ups are surrounded by hoards of friends or colleagues though. Not every grown up is an extrovert, but they're also not an island. They look for and hold multiple perspectives from the connections that they make in the world. They support and are supported by others, whether that's other people, animals or nature. And, importantly, they're in connection with themselves. They have an understanding of themselves. No one can ever be entirely self-aware but what we do notice is that grown ups are forever trying to know themselves better.

> *'I define connection as the energy that exists between people when they feel seen, heard, and valued; when they can give and receive without judgment; and when they derive sustenance and strength from the relationship.'*
> **Brené Brown**

A key enabler of connection is Compassion - the second practice of a grown up. Reaching out with compassion, looking for compassion in moments that are tense, sad, anger fuelled, awkward or dangerous. Sending your compassion toward other people, and hugging yourself with it at times too. Compassion allows us to recognise the complexity of being human, however inconvenient that can be at times. Believing that there is always more going on for ourselves and for others than we can ever know.

> *'Our task must be to free ourselves by widening our circle of compassion to embrace all living creatures and the whole of nature and its beauty.'*
> **Albert Einstein**

But being compassionate can at times take Vulnerability - the third practice of a grown up. Vulnerability means opening ourselves up, trying things, risking things, asking things. And it's in this space of vulnerability that we have seen people grow and stretch and develop and connect. Smiling at a stranger is a risk, it leaves us vulnerable to rejection - but is it a risk worth taking for a smile back? Is it a risk worth taking for the potential to make someone's day? Is it a risk worth taking to give someone the only moment of connection they may have in their day, or week, or year? Vulnerability is a strong magnet and it will pull people toward us - we must be careful how we use it!

> *'When we were children, we used to think that when we were grown-up we would no longer be vulnerable. But to grow up is to accept vulnerability... To be alive is to be vulnerable.'*
> **Madeleine L'Engle**

The fourth practice, and one that I know you are already practicing if you've got this far, is Curiosity. Grown ups look to understand more. While they value and respect their expertise, and recognise how it may form and inform their identity, they know it is not all that they are. There is a whole world out there that they can't be an expert in. In fact, in the small village cafe that I am currently sitting and typing in there is a world of unknown. I don't know what is in my green tea. And if I learnt the ingredients, I still wouldn't know the process to dry them. Or the room and equipment needed. I don't know what the waiter is scared of, or the food that makes the chef smile, or the lifetime of moments that led the two older gentlemen on the table next to me to cycle here today. I don't know and I will never know - and isn't that exciting!

> *'I don't know anything, but I do know that everything is interesting if you go into it deeply enough.'*
> **Richard Feynman**

Connection, Compassion, Vulnerability and Curiosity - Four practices of a grown up. Four practices that none of us need to wait another moment to try.

What I find incredible in my learning, and laughable really, is the tension between the grown up game I took part in for so long, and the grown up I am practicing being now. And how the two, from the outside, may not always look that different.

When playing the grown up game I tried to look and be strong on my own - needing no-one. The irony of this stance is that connection strengthens us, and is an evolutionary need in us as humans - we are pack animals. That's not to say we can't be our own person, but if we live our entire lives like that and build fences and walls around us, we'll struggle to be a grown up, and we may struggle to be truly happy. The most laughable part? When I practice being in connection with others I feel stronger and likely appear so too.

When I was playing the grown up game I felt that compassion, particularly for myself, was weak. I thought it was soft. I saw any kind of compassion for self as self pity and I rarely allowed myself to feel aggrieved by others - surely I was avoiding my accountability if I felt myself a victim? I thought compassion circumnavigated accountability. It didn't fit with the demanding stereotype that I thought it was to be a grown up. But I had double standards: I was full of compassion for others, just none for myself. The irony here being that I now see compassion as a superpower. Compassion has been my most effective tool in conflict, in liberating myself from angst and anger toward others and toward myself. Compassion is a muscle - and it too makes me feel strong.

And vulnerability - well, I didn't understand it. When playing the grown up game, vulnerability felt like a weakness. It was too big a risk to open myself up and let people see what was really going on. My grown up mask was thickest in covering my vulnerabilities. And yet, now I find that being a grown up is all about vulnerability, and that change simply can't happen without it. Only when we let go of one thing can we move toward another, but letting go takes vulnerability. Only when we show how we truly feel or truly think can we connect authentically, but showing ourselves takes vulnerability. Only when we name the present can we work toward a different future, but you've guessed it, acknowledging the present takes vulnerability. Vulnerability isn't weak - it's a courageous catalyst for change.

The last tension, the last laughable, absurd irony is that when I was playing the grown up game I thought that certainty was imperative. Grown ups have the answers. Grown ups are experts. Grown ups know. And now I find that curiosity is king: recognising that we don't have the answers, that certainty is far rarer than we think. And that walking towards things that we don't understand is a way of inviting others to join us. Certainty is misguided in most situations. There are very few 'right' ways of doing things, or of being. Accepting that we can't know most things and instead wandering around the world wondering is a practice of a grown up.

We can visualise these aspects of being a grown up as a human body, moving confidently through the world. We steady ourselves and move forward with legs of Vulnerability and Curiosity. We reach out with arms of Compassion and for Connection. There are two further aspects of a grown up that are both a practice and an outcome. When practicing vulnerability, curiosity, compassion and connection, we increase our awareness of ourselves, others and the world - we can picture the head of our beautiful grown up ever filling with Consciousness. And then let's travel down from the head into the chest, to the heart space, where our sixth practice tends to reside - Choice. Grown ups have more choices, or at least they notice their choices more often and make them consciously.

So here is our joyful grown up:

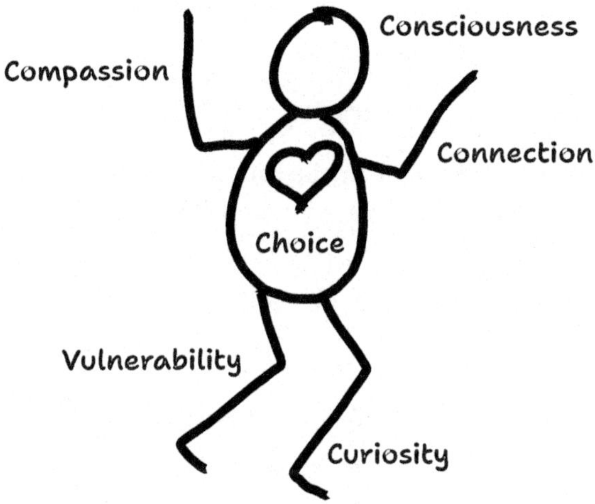

If we lean toward all of this, if we look to create connections, if we practice our compassion, if we share our vulnerabilities openly and if we step forward with curiosity, we will have greater awareness and consciousness of the world. We will feel less vulnerable. We will feel more connected. We will feel even more curious because the more we learn, the more we will realise we don't know. And we will understand people and things more deeply and have greater compassion for all. There's that mayonnaise again!

We will unlock choices we never knew we had. We will be better equipped to make conscious, more informed, more open, more inviting choices about how we are, how we want to be. Grown ups, even just for a split second, appear to have more choice. They seem to have a choice between what they hold tightly and what they hold lightly. When we are grown ups, which I remind you, I don't think anyone is all of the time, we can choose how we want to be.

And remember, the beautiful thing about this is that all of these practices feed into and off of one another. Practicing grown upness is not linear. It's not a process of moving from one thing to another; it's emulsified eggs and oil.

I can choose to be more curious, which in itself may unlock compassion, which in itself may allow me to be vulnerable and create a deeper connection with someone. By only enacting my compassion, I may soon find that I'm curious. By simply going out and looking for connections, I'm sure to raise my consciousness and have choices crop up in front of my eyes. It may be in noticing a lack of curiosity that we notice a choice, in a moment that lacks compassion we stretch for connections, in noticing our self-preservation we choose vulnerability.

And breathe.

I'm noticing myself and my demeanour shifting as I am writing this, as I am drawing the circle from where I started and where I am now.

In describing these tensions, these shifts from the grown up game to a grown up practice I am noticing an opening up.

My body feels like it has gone from holding my breath in to exhaling loudly, my arms have moved from crossing my body to being wide open. I have moved from hoping to be seen as tall and controlled, a contorted and tight grown up, to truly being a person showing all that I am to the world and wanting to see all that the world is too.

I am more spacious. My chest is not concave and protected but high and open and vulnerable. My face is not pinched, furrowed with seriousness but bright, happy and safe for others to come close to. My shoulders are loose, my hands relaxed, my heart awake. I can breathe. I am not performing the game of adulthood, but practicing being grown up.

When I am a grown up, when I am myself, I can breathe - and I can choose the rhythm of that breath.

So let's try this definition on for size...

Grown up

Noun/Adjective

A person who actively practices compassion, curiosity, vulnerability and creates connections - and practices these in regard to themselves, others and the world around them - resulting in ever expanding consciousness and an ever increasing array of choices.

'Sammy has embarked on grown up practices.'

'I parent like a grown up - with compassion and curiosity, recognising that I have choices.'

'Gemma can't wait to see what opportunities practising being a grown up may unleash!'

CHAPTER 14

Prompts for our practice

I'm mindful at this point not to launch into 'tips and tricks' of being a grown up - it's clearly not that simple - but I do want to pause and suggest just a few ways that we may all practice a little, or spot opportunities to practice.

Firstly, if choice is a big part of it then rest assured, we are already making around 33–35,000 choices a day, although the vast majority are unconscious. So we just need to bring a few more of those to the fore and make them more consciously. And, conveniently, many of those will be choices about the other practices.

Secondly, the more we practice, the easier it will get. While our brain isn't a muscle it can work like one. The more we use neural pathways, the more the brain recognises them as well worn and easy routes to travel. If we consciously exercise compassion it doesn't take long for it to become second nature. If we push ourselves to ask curious questions we'll soon find ourselves holding more and more facts lightly. So practice may not make perfect, but practice does make practice easier.

Here are some questions that prompt and promote my grown up practice:

- **What is going on for me right now?**
  Can I name my feelings? Am I defensive or protective? Have I become consumed by this stance? Am I still listening or am I hearing what I want to hear? Am I happy, sad, angry, excited, nervous, doubtful, scared?

- **How do I want to be right now?**
  When I look back on this moment or this relationship, later - how do I want to have been? What would make me proud? How possible is that for me? What do I need to make it a reality?

- **What don't I know?**
  There is always more going on that we are aware of. Just walking through all of the possibilities can help me to loosen my grip on the 'reality' I have decided upon. What context do I understand and what may I never know?

- **What might that person need right now that I could gift them?**
  All of our feelings emerge from need; a met need or an unmet need. What do I, or the other party, need right now? A smile, a shoulder, a comrade, forgiveness, acceptance, an invitation, to be seen, to be heard, or space.

- **What could be possible for us if I move toward them (emotionally)?**
  If I were to safely attempt to meet their need, or create a space in which they can meet it themselves could they be lifted? Could I be lifted? Could we be together? Might they feel safe? Might they be more themselves? Might I?

- **What's the absolute worst that could happen right now?**
  This is probably the question I head to first. When I am in a good space, and with practice, I can often gallop through the others

either quickly or subconsciously, but this one is a gem - rarely the worst that could happen is actually that bad! And often if the worst that could happen is someone else's reaction - it probably says more about them than about you. So what's the worst that could happen, and how likely is that?

- **What choices are available to me?**
  So what then? Do I choose to act? Or do I choose not to act? It is important to remember that both are a choice - inaction is still a choice. Push yourself to really consider all of your options, even the silly ones.

One last pearl of wisdom, if I may - and this is a pearl that has been given to me by others many times over. Don't try to become an expert at grown upness overnight. Pianists don't start out with Beethoven. Surgeons aren't given heart patients on day one. Chefs wash up first, Comedians start in local pubs, Toddlers have their first steps. Simply deciding to be a full-on grown up tomorrow will likely fail. Instead look for a little, manageable thing to practice on.

If you know of a person who needs to be seen, see them - say good morning, that's all for now. If a friend has gone quiet and not answered you back - message again, let them know you are here when they need you. If you aren't making time for what you need to be happy or healthy, find five minutes to have a chat with yourself - what do you really need?

Think of something that scares you, something small and manageable - a conversation you've been avoiding perhaps, a dish that you've been reluctant to cook, just telling someone how you really are when they ask. Something small that feels a tiny bit risky - do it and see how it goes. What's the worst that could happen?

If people walking slowly on the pavement infuriates you, reach for your compassion - perhaps they are enjoying their journey, perhaps they have a bad leg, perhaps they don't want to go where they are headed. If your partner snaps at you after a busy day, reach for your compassion and offer it to them overtly. If you hear your inner critic pipe up when you make a mistake - thank them for trying to keep you safe.

If tomorrow you have a meeting in which you know you will want to be seen as the expert, dial up your curiosity - make a point of wondering what you might learn if you ask questions of others. How might their opinions shift the way you see things? How might that improve everything? Or promise yourself that the next time someone uses a word or acronym you don't know you will ask for clarity.

Notice the next time you think there are no choices, even in a tiny inconsequential moment, notice your fixed and narrow mindset and challenge yourself to think of three possible options available to you.

In the first instance, your practice may only stretch to noticing. Noticing opportunities, noticing the absence of these practices, noticing how you feel. Then move on to trying stuff out...

CHAPTER 15

Something is missing

As I draw my exploration to a close, for today at least, I notice an itch that hasn't been scratched. I am aware of something that feels incredibly important to me in how I practice my grown upness and yet it hasn't been drawn out in our definition. I wonder if, ironically, the grown up game stopped me. I know I've been had by it at times when writing this book. This aspect or quality did show up in many of our stories and reflections however, and is definitely something that I have been able to better access and give attention to since I have begun my grown up practice.

Play.

Ironically, when I was *playing* the grown up game it didn't feel like play - it felt like a performance. Perhaps it was like being *in* a play.

What I am now referring to is the joyous act of playing. Games with no consequences, play with no *real* winners or losers; wordplay, quizzes, netball, sudoku, lego, jenga, jokes, cards, eye spy, banter, would you rather, trivial pursuit, and more - play for the sake of play.

And even playfulness - bringing lightness to my work, creativity to the dull, laughter to the serious. Play is hugely important to me, and yet I can often forget how much I need it in my life.

A couple of years ago I was really busy with work stuff and family. I was travelling a lot and in truth I was burning myself out. I was always tired unless I was facilitating client work, from which I would get a boost of adrenaline then crash soon after. In bed, rather than sleep I was doom scrolling, I was checking emails rather than playing with the kids and the majority of my conversations were serious and consequential - nothing was light.

At one point in the summer, I spotted an event in my diary. I'd been away most of the week travelling around the UK, I was tired and hoping for a relaxed and low key weekend (with my phone and social apps probably). My heart sank when I realised my Saturday was committed to a village social event.

On the day I did my usual, sucked it up, put on my best extroverted face and herded Jim and the boys to the cricket pitch for a game of rounders. Long story short - it was awesome, just what I needed!

Not being in charge, not having an agenda or a job other than to take part was like medicine. I hit balls, I fielded, I trotted around the bases with my toddler in arms after he whacked a ball, I cheered people on, I barbed the opposition. Then it was on to the tug of war which I threw myself into and lost miserably; then we quickly transitioned to the egg toss - another life giving loss amongst friends and strangers. The hoard of us then headed to the village hall for a BBQ while the kids coordinated an impromptu 'show' on the stage - which, to my surprise, all our kind neighbours attended.

I went home from that village social revitalised. Inconsequential play has given me what I needed - a chance to relax while feeling active.

Whether it's the banter between friends or the gamification of tidying up. Whether it's making time for netball or inviting clients to laugh while we work, play feels like the gift of a grown up. We can choose to take life seriously, or we can seriously choose to play.

I now choose the latter.

EPILOGUE

So am I a grown up?

This has been a huge exploration for me. Since starting the book I have had a second child, nearly split up with my partner, returned to playing netball, worked with hundreds of people in organisations, started a new business, interviewed tens of people about being grown up and about meaningful and important moments in their lives. I have lost people. I have gained people. I have lived my life.

And I have definitely lived it with all of the learnings I have gathered along the way.

So, am I a grown up now?

Well, sometimes.

It is a practice that never ends.

Notes

Rites of Passage
Grayson Perry. Swan Films for Channel 4. UK. *Pg. 37*

Preferential Detachment During Human Brain Development
Sol Lim; Cheol E. Han; Peter J. Uhlhaas; Marcus Kaiser. *Pg. 43*

Brain Architecture
Center on the Developing Child, Harvard University. Pg. 44

Average age of first time mothers in the UK
Office for National Statistics. Pg. 47

Strengthen relationships for longer, healthier life
Harvard Health Publishing. Pg. 58

Loneliness, Social Isolation, and Cardiovascular Health
Ning Xia 1, Huige Li. Pg. 58

The risks of social isolation
Amy Novotney. Pg. 58

Getting the Message Out: Media Context and Global Changes in Attitudes toward Homosexuality
Phillip Ayoub and Jeremiah Garretson. Pg. 62

Shift in divorce rates
Office for National Statistics. Pg. 72

How Couple's Relationship Lasts Over Time? A Model for Marital Satisfaction
José Abreu-Afonso, Maria Meireles Ramos, Inês Queiroz-Garcia, Isabel Leal, William James Center for Research, Instituto Universitário, Lisbon, Portugal. Pg. 72

Psychology Today - Big 5 Personality Traits
Pg. 91

Your future self
Hal Hershfield, University of California, Los Angeles. Pg. 92

Immune Neglect: A source of Durability Bias in Affective Forecasting
Gilbert, Wilson, Pinel and Blumberg, University of Virginia. Pg. 93

The Harvard Happiness Study
Pg. 114

Nicomachean Ethics
Aristotle. Pg. 116

The characteristics of a high performance organization
André de Waal, HPO Center, the Netherlands. Pg. 151

State of the global workplace report
Gallup's 2025. Pg. 152

Transactional Analysis in Psychotherapy
Eric Berne. Pg. 154

Stanford Prison Experiment
(also known as the Zimbardo Prison Experiment). Naval Research Reviews and American Psychologist. Pg. 163

The Kindness Test
Sussex Centre for Research on Kindness. University of Sussex. Pg. 176

The World Happiness Report 2025
Pg. 176

Child-care practices anteceding three patterns of preschool behavior. Genetic Psychology Monographs
Baumrind, D. Pg. 194

The influence of parenting style on adolescent competence and substance use. Journal of Early Adolescence
Baumrind, D. Pg. 194

Child Development Theories: For Parents & Educators
Gwen Dewar Pg. 194

Socialization in the context of the family: Parent–child interaction. In P. H. Mussen & E. M. Hetherington, Handbook of child psychology: Vol. 4. Socialization, personality, and social development (4th ed.)
Maccoby, E. E., & Martin, J. A. (1983). New York. Pg. 195

The role of parents in the socialization of children: An historical overview. Developmental Psychology
Maccoby, E.E. (1992). Pg. 195

Day-to-day Consistency in Positive Parent–Child Interactions and Youth Well-Being.
Lippold, M. Chandler, K. Lawson, K. McHale, S 2016. Pg. 196

Printed in Dunstable, United Kingdom

68828854R00141